UNSUNG HEROES

Deconstructing Suicide

Through Stories of Triumph

Compiled by Kristie Knights

For more information, visit www.kristieknights.com or
www.iriseleadership.com

Book and cover design by Jennifer Insignares
www.yourdesignsbyjen.com

Edited by Amanda Horan
www.amandahoranediting.weebly.com

Formatted by Bojan Kratofil

Publishing House UnSung Hero Publishing
Publishing House 9400 McKnight Road, Suite 201 Pittsburgh PA, 15237

ISBN: 978-1-5136-1729-9

Dedication

To my children: Madalyn, Kamron, and Katie.

May the world be a kinder and gentler place as a result of the vulnerability and courage of each unsung hero in this book, and books to come in the future.

Appreciation

With deepest thanks…

It is with the deepest of gratitude that I thank you Lisa Mack-Finn, for being you! Thank you for your courage, vulnerability, and wisdom at the darkest time in your life. You have and will continue to inspire others to live! I am grateful for your friendship and love! Thank you for the inspiration of UnSung Heroes, and the amazing non-profit 501 (c)(3), iRise Leadership Institute. Together, we will eradicate suicide.

Through hours of toil and labor, silently and fervently my husband Tom, stood by. In days of despair or discouragement he has been unwavering. In the days of triumph and joyful moments he has provided love and passion for those I have grown to hold in high esteem; the unsung heroes of this book; of the books to come in the future. He has been my rock, refuge, and wind beneath my wings. I do love and cherish you, my soulmate, best friend, and partner in life, my husby, Tom Knights.

Madalyn, Kamron, and Katie I praise and thank God each day for each of you. The hours are long, the sacrifices have been many for each of you. At times I have not been available or present for you. Quietly and intentionally, each of you have said "It is ok." My greatest gift to you is the knowledge that through Christ all things *are* possible. My desire is to make a better world for them; a world less hidden, full of shame. A world of love, acceptance, and freedom to 'just be.' I love you with all of my heart. Each and every moment I give is in service to you and your beautiful future. Thank you for unconditionally supporting this journey, supporting me.

I am in awe of the Board of iRise Leadership Institute and friends. They are synonymous. I am so very thankful for the unwavering support of the first of many book projects. Their belief in my vision, mission, crazy, risky, impulsive, we-will-do-it attitude!! I am grateful to you Katie Vollen, Scott Cunningham, Cindy Steinhauser, Kerrie Boydman, Chelsea Thokar, Mark Lutz, Jennifer Glassbrenner, and especially my dearest friend Paula Miles.

Paula, thank you for loving me through the highs and lows, impulsive, insane, and tragic moments in my life. I do love you! You have been an unconditional friend and colleague. I feel so blessed and thankful to share leadership on the Board of iRise with you! Thank you for not only serving as the Vice President, but also as my greatest friend!

Thank you to my parents for their unwavering and eternal love. It was in my darkest days and most joyous moments they have stood vigil and faithful to who I was, am, and will be! None of this would be possible without you both!! I love you so very much!

I want to thank Attorney Victoria Kush, and the law firm Buchanan, Ingersoll, and Rooney. Victoria, thank you for your legal guidance in the establishment of the contract for the Contributing Authors. I will always remember the day we shared lunch. You looked at me and said, establish a non-profit. There will be greater success long term. The embers of passion ignited. You and your law firm pledged to provide legal consultation and contract creation for no cost. Buchanan, Ingersoll, and Rooney, thank you for your gracious donation!

Yes, a Facebook post may have ignited this vision; but it was my dear friend and colleague Shellie Hipsky, the founder of GlobalSisterhood 501 (c)(3) Non-Profit, which I am the vice president, that created the space for the vision. As I felt lost, and wondering, she opened her home for a meal. We spent the afternoon vision boarding. Although I struggled to share my desire to serve others *and* be recognized for my efforts; she looked at me and said 'you are worthy. Put it on the Board. Do it.' I did. I thank you Shellie for believing in me.

The mission of the Global Sisterhood: the Global Sisterhood educates while providing resources and networking for women and girls internationally. By forming connections and supporting each other's missions, movements, we will provide sustainable ways for women throughout the world to make their goals and dreams a reality.

My Angel, Kate Gardner (mentor and coach) and The Missing Piece Team; which includes Jennifer Insignares (graphic designer), Amanda Horan (editor), and Bojan Kratofil (formatting), I am forever grateful to you. As many authors, I believe in this book; this project. I had no doubts that it would be fully funded and then some with a Kickstarter campaign. As the deadline neared, my anxiety rose. *What will I do? I have so many counting on the publication of this book.* I felt overwhelmed; still determined, but overwhelmed with worry.

Just a few days prior to the end of the Kickstarter, Kate sent a private message to me (which she shared in the foreword). I was speechless, literally. I could not believe there would be someone so kind to finance this project. Honestly, it took days for me to grasp the gracious gift from Kate and her Team. There was an entire team of beautiful people willing to donate their time and talents to the publication of this book. I am on my knees thankful for each of you!

In addition, Kate Gardner, *the* Kate, would be my coach, my mentor! Kate, I do love you so very much! I am inspired daily by who you are as a woman, grandmother, mother, coach, and leader. It is through you lives have been and will continue to be saved! I am so very thankful for you in my professional *and* personal life as a friend.

Most importantly, I thank you dearest Jesus. Many nights I lay awake, searching, and your unwavering and unconditional presence was clear to me. Often I clung to Psalm 46:10 which states: be still and know that I am God. Nothing has been more clear to me than His presence in my journey. Thank you dear Jesus with the honor to serve each and every person who will be touched by this life.

Table of Contents

Foreword

I was watching Kristie out the corner of my eye, watching her start on the road to her dream of something huge and life changing. It kind of reminded me of myself 3 years ago when I first became a best-selling author. I too had set out with a huge dream in my heart of creating a platform for people to share their stories with the world. I had my first taste of what it was like to be a co-author of a best-selling book and now I wanted to be the person who created the platform for others, only I failed. I failed dramatically on a worldwide level.

With 15 authors signed up to my project, no funds and nowhere to go I sat in the corner and cried out to God one day. I said "God, please help me, you wanted me to create this, now you give me the help I need to finish it."

Sure, enough, as he always stays true, he did just that. My publisher took the book back to the drawing board and re-named it: The Missing Piece: A Transformational Journey and placed a new cover on the front.

On Dec 7th, 2013 my book became a #1 international bestseller and it led me on one astounding journey, one that 3 years later has helped me become a 17 times best-selling author, build a successful company, be named as one of the most influential coaches in the world, help nearly 200 authors become best-selling authors and become the editor of a magazine.

Now, here we were 3 years later with a carbon copy of myself in front of me called Kristie Knights, begging to God to help her, to show her a sign of mercy to help make her dream come alive. I knew it was my duty to help her, just like I had that helping hand 3 years ago. Nothing happens by accident and when somebody presents themselves to you in need it is up to you to help them.

I sent Kristie a message and give her two options:

1. I will donate $100 to your cause and just walk away.

Or

2. I will donate $100 to your cause plus $10,000 worth of my expertise, ask my team to work for less and publish your book by Christmas 2016, what do you say?

I can only imagine this ladies Christmases came all at once when I said this to her. To no longer need to struggle to find the funds to make the book happen must have felt like a tonne weight had been lifted from her shoulders. Also, to give hope to every one of the authors in this book too really is truly an honor to be sent by God himself to help make this happen for all of them.

Never take praying to God for granted, he does listen and will send you a solution, even if it is in some crazy amazing way he will still send it when you ask. Which is exactly what Kristie has now experienced by praying daily her dreams were answered.

So, here's to one amazing journey for Kristie Knights and may her journey be as amazing as mine has.

Much love and appreciation

Kate Gardner

17 x Best Selling Author & Editor of The Missing Piece Magazine

www.themissingpiecemagazine.com

Introduction

I lay in bed wondering. *What is my purpose? How can I make a larger impact on this world? What is my legacy? How do I want my children to view and remember me?* It was a moment of self-doubt. It was a moment where I was not able to get out of bed. The motivation, inspiration, and expectations had dissipated. I must admit, I was worried, I felt lost. Yes, even as a psychotherapist and leader in the community, I have my moments too. I know, you're surprised. The expectation is I will always be full, ready to give. Lead. Strong. Serve others. I am human. In that moment, I felt lost.

Aimlessly I turned off the alarm; hitting snooze a third time. I continued to scroll through Facebook; another reminder I am not enough. Professional accolades abound. Although I will admit, I have achieved so much in service to others. I still felt empty…

What is a hero to you? Often a person who serves in the military comes to mind. Or perhaps a mentor in your life? Daily, I share space with the unsung heroes in our world.

I listen to pain, loneliness, feelings of inadequacy, and despair. Secrets are divulged. Lies uncovered. Crimes of the heart confessed. As I listen, my heart breaks when I hear many that do not feel they are worthy of life, not worthy to live, breath…life. They search for significance in this world, their world; in my space. What more can I do?

Depression, anxiety, domestic violence, sexual abuse, panic attacks, rejection, abandonment, and shame. Cloaked in pain, defeating gremlins; each enter back into the word masked in shame. But you see, when I look at each and every person I encounter, I see the hero within. I see the daily, perhaps hourly battles they have survived; thrived. They are not defined as a 'mental case,' 'weak,' 'broken' or 'crazy.' They are an unsung hero. Each person is a warrior of life. The learn to survive despite the brokenness. In fact, they learn to thrive, leveraging the pain! Instead of their story bringing shame; in *UnSung Heroes*, it brings strength, empowerment, and purposeful living!

Enter the world of beautiful people who have chosen life. They have surmounted the pain. They have battled, and won. In these pages are the darkest of moments for each person. You have the unique gift to share in the dankest of pain, yet the joy of the rise. With courage and vulnerability, each author describes the chains that bound them, from mental illness, suicidal thoughts, to suicidal attempts. Allow the tears to flow. Do not squelch the emotion. Permit vulnerability, as you rise through their stories.

According to the American Foundation for Suicide Prevention:

- On average there are 117 suicides per day.

- Each day 23 veterans die by suicide.

- Suicide is the 10th leading cause of death in the US.

- Each year 42,773 Americans die by suicide.

- More teenagers and young adults die from suicide than from cancer, heart disease, AIDS, birth defects, strokes, pneumonia, influenza, and chronic lung disease *combined*.

Whether you have lost a loved one to suicide, have suicidal thoughts, or have attempted suicide; this book will engage you, enrage you, bring you to your knees, and empower you! These unsung heroes portray a story of triumph despite the odds. They will teach us how to laugh, love, and thrive again! Shame and stigma of mental illness, suicidal thoughts, and attempts will be lifted through the journeys of each author. Lives will be saved.

I did not know Lisa Mack-Finn; although there she was on my Facebook feed. I am sure she was one of the thousands I friended to 'increase' my likes. Her post read of her journey after a traumatic brain injury; a concussion had resulted in depression and ultimately, suicidal thoughts.

Her post was bathed in pain. I read the words of a moment she made a choice. Looking at the pills on the dresser, hearing her children play in the next room; longing to end the pain. It was as if I was in that moment with her. I could relate to the loneliness, the emotional pain of a life experience. She chose life. She chose to echo the words of purposeful living. In a snippet of her journey lie the words that shifted my world, my being. I am in deepest gratitude for you Lisa Mack-Finn. Your vulnerability and courage has inspired this project, which became the non-profit iRise Leadership Institute. It has led to the saving of many lives. I am thankful for you!

"The night I envisioned killing myself was the night I began a list of all the things I was worthy and deserving of."

-Lisa Mack-Finn

A simple post, a simple quote changed everything. You see, there is something to be said for a group of people coming together for a common purpose. There is also something to be said for the strength that comes from vulnerability. Within these pages are true stories of unsung heroes, heroes that have decided to share their journey in hopes that their words may also resonate with someone who is struggling. We hope that our stories will inspire, guide and lift up those that need to rise. We come from all walks of life, but share a common thread.

Suicide should not be a word that is feared or suppressed any longer. What brings a person to that point of being so low that the only option, the only thought would be to end the pain? We have shed light on this question and we asked our authors to tell us how they triumphed through it all.

Many unsung heroes remain quiet, small; still in fear of being judged or misunderstood. Our goal is to lift that stigma, to uncover answers so that we all can have a better understanding in order to deconstruct suicide.

Every day we turn on the news we hear more stories of children, teens and adults ending their lives. We watch as families grieve and ask *why*. Our mission as writers and survivors has come full circle with the help of our friend Kristie Knights.

Kristie has served as an inspiration and leader to many of us who needed a voice. After seeing the quote, I had written recounting a night I struggled with suicidal thoughts, Kristie knew that she needed to do something. She began the iRise Leadership Institute, an organization whose main mission was to educate, bring awareness to and eradicate suicide. Through each other we learned that words have power; that a simple online post could not only inspire the formation of a non-profit organization, but also give the unsung heroes a voice and platform to share and heal. We respect the strength and courage it took to share these stories so that we can learn and understand the *why*.

"When I awoke the next morning, my outlook was clearer and I had a renewed sense of purpose and strength. My rising into this day was a huge milestone from the proceeding night of desperation and loneliness."

-Lisa Mack-Finn

It's in the silent moments when you're alone, no one there to fill
a home,

nothin' especially bad, just the moment's tone

Your mind starts to drift & before you know it you're wonderin'
if,

if I hadn't done this or would have said that

would I be here now, be where I'm at?

But you've gotta believe, have faith, stay strong,

& know you'll carry on

Just believe it on & on & on…

Spin your wheels, grind your gears,

exhaust your engine while you search for redemption

You're not standin' still, though it might seem so

You're wherever you need to be,

even if the reason is one you can't see

But you've gotta believe, have faith, stay strong,

& know you'll carry on

Just believe it on & on & on…

UnSung Heroes

Stuck in the mud, feel helpless in life's rut,

tryin' to take yourself away, find better luck

To run isn't the answer, nowhere for you to go,

You have to stick it out even when you feel so low

Look up, look out, look within,

hold your head high, keep up your chin

It's gonna keep comin', like it or not,

life happens every second, puts you in a whole new spot

Circumstances are just that & control is something you don't have,

even in grief you have to remember to dance

Because you have the power to get through,

heart, determination, & all that's within you

But you've gotta believe, have faith, stay strong,

& know you'll carry on

Just believe it on & on & on…

Yes believe, have faith, stay strong, & know you'll carry on

And so iRise…

I rise above the ashes & out of the shadows

I rise above the clouds, elated & not looking down

I rise above the feeling, I do not want to die

I rise into the sunshine, feel it on my face

I rise to greet others & give them an embrace

I rise to be better, strive to be more

I rise to be the eagle, spreading its wings to soar

I rise to be a winner, achieving all my dreams

I rise to be a good person, saying what I mean

And so iRise…

-Jessica D. Comer

Chapter 1

The Prelude to -Unknown

by Lisa Mack-Finn

I write about it in my book; I write about the night I envisioned swallowing a bottle of pills. At the time I put the book together, I wasn't able to share in writing all of the details of that night. It took me almost one year to release this draft. These words sat on my computer for months just waiting patiently for their turn to be shared. See, I am watching the world unfold around me with people committing suicide in record numbers. I am watching us watching it unfold. I hear the comments being made, judgments and concerns. I have been listening and taking notes. I have been sitting here thinking that I could have been another sad news story. Mother of three, swallowed a bottle of pills. Who knew? Why did she do it? Why did she leave us? Why didn't she ask for help? Why? Why? Why? Maybe we ought to hear from those of us who thought about putting an end to the pain-but didn't. Who in the hell wants to actually talk about it? I didn't, until now. There are so many misconceptions…she must be depressed, crazy, selfish, lazy, or abused. If I offer my readers the opportunity to see how the night unfolded, maybe a little clarity will help unfold the why's. Or, maybe not, but I can tell you that what I have learned in writing -*Unknown* is that you never know who you will help, inspire or enlighten through writing. Let me put you in that room with me now, shall I?

That night, my husband at the time, walked through the bathroom, which is connected to my bedroom. He couldn't see me as I held my head in pain, lifting it ever so much and squinting to see his face. I said very simply, "I think I want to kill myself. I can't take this pain anymore." The words came out of my mouth very matter of fact. I may have used the word seriously. "I seriously want to kill myself." It was something along those lines. There wasn't anything to it, simple as that. In that moment, I turned my gaze from the bottle of pills to the well-lit bathroom, waiting for his response. I wanted to feel something. I wanted to feel love. He turned off the light in the bathroom and responded, "Don't do that" and walked out shutting the door behind him. He never hesitated in his stride and was very calm, as if I told him I was going to make a cup of tea.

The moment the door shut I leaned back slowly into my pillows which felt like bricks beneath my injured head. Nothing would harbor me from the pain, not my husband, not even my pillows. I hurt. I hurt from the inside out with a feeling of abandonment and pain. Having a head injury felt like I was stuck in a world that simply didn't understand how badly I physically hurt because they couldn't see my pain. I didn't want to burden anyone any longer. I didn't want to share and feel out loud because I felt I was annoying. I desperately wanted to be well again. *Don't do that.* I hung on to those words in my mind and teetered on angry and sad, angry and sad. I stared at the pills. I needed a reprieve, a moment of wellness and no pain. I was hyper focused on how my injury was affecting everyone else. How my state of being was a nuisance. I hated that I felt segregated from my family and I hated that they didn't know what to do with me in this state. I felt like I was not in control of me. I didn't like feeling out of control.

Don't do that, I repeated to myself as I curled up tight- sobbing. I kept saying it over and over in my head as I began to cry out loud. I remember very clearly silencing myself, as if my grief was not worthy of being heard. Let me say that again. I remember silencing myself, as if my grief was not worthy of being heard. I stared at the pills.

My kids were outside of the bedroom door in the family room, playing and watching TV. Life was going on outside of my four walls. Life was moving on loudly and brilliantly, and all without me. I lay quiet and still, just listening to them for quite some time.

In my stillness, an overload of emotions and feeling began to gather and create what I now call fuel. This was my inner strength showing me up and telling my body to rise up. I focused on my childrens' voices. I swallowed my tears and felt that huge weight of nothing within my throat that ached as I tried to breathe. My tears flowed and I cried out loud looking up to the ceiling. I did not silence myself this time as I grieved and I gave myself the opportunity to be real and raw and feel what my heart and mind wanted to feel. I began to settle. I did this for quite some time.

I reached for the phone to call my sister and her words of encouragement along with the compassion and empathy that she shared enveloped me. Over the hour, I became empowered in the environment around me. I gathered myself together, wiping the tears on my face with my robe, and slowly sat up. I breathed in and out as if it were rehearsed and swung my legs to the side of the bed. My head fell forward as I bit my bottom lip in pain and stood up slowly. My body from the neck down was fine, but each movement created vibrations into my damaged brain that I was endlessly trying to avoid. I reached to the left and flipped on the light. I abruptly shut my eyes because it was too bright. I dimmed the switch and began walking slowly towards the bottle of pills. I felt as though I could hear my heart beating in my head which made me dizzy. The dizziness created nausea, an endless cycle I had been experiencing. With my left hand, I reached for the bottle and gripped it strongly while stabilizing my body with my right hand. My kids' laughter echoed in my head, and as their world moved forward, I wanted to be a part of it. I closed my eyes and prayed one of my very first –Unknowns.

"Jesus, thank you for giving me the strength to see that I am worthy and deserving of so much more. Let me continue to find the strength to rise up and get well for my children."

- Lisa Mack-Finn

I still pray that prayer most days and I still have that bottle on my dresser as a memento of sorts, like a shell I found at the beach, it elicits a feeling inside of me. The feeling now is not of fear but of hope.

I say that writing saved my life and it did. But, I would be lying to all of my readers if I didn't share that my ex-husband's words saved my life. My childrens' footsteps and laughter outside of my bedroom saved my life. My sister saved my life. More importantly, I saved my life.

On a daily basis we have to be still and look around us to see what we can use as our fuel. What is the reason, who is the reason that you rise up every day? How are you going to relinquish the control that no longer harbors you and succumb to the hand you have been dealt? The world will go on with or without us so plan your rise up to the world. Your fuel will come when you give yourself permission to grieve out loud and extinguish the fires of untruths that are echoing around you and in your head. Grieving out loud, it is ok to grieve out loud. Your fuel will come when you recognize that you are worthy and deserving of so much more than your current state of dismay or the physical, emotional or psychological pain and stress that is crippling you. Your fuel will come in as strength in tiny bits and pieces or in one big crashing wave like it did for me. It doesn't matter, but trust me, at the very bottom of your barrel, and we all have bottoms to our barrels, you have the ability to find fuel. I believe that. You are more. Find your fuel daily and you too, will rise.

Chapter 2

Ripple Effect

by Laura Dahl

"As for you, you meant evil against me,

but God meant it for good,

to bring it about that many people

should be kept alive, as they are today."

- Genesis 50:20

I begin my chapter with this verse from the Bible because it is my life verse that God has given me. The things that could have destroyed me are the very things that God has not only used but *meant* it for good. This is the moment he has appointed and anointed for me to share this piece of my story and potentially save the lives of many. I pray it brings glory to God, who has given me purpose and sustained me for this life that is so much more than I could have ever imagined.

Let me give you some insight into my mind. Negative thoughts were always in my head, and it was as if I had no control over them. They would come out of nowhere. I never felt good enough. These thoughts were trying to persuade me to end my life, and they were very compelling. Throughout every attempt of suicide I experienced, I cannot say there was an active decision process made on my part. During the several attempts growing up, I always remember crying as it happened, as if I did not truly want to die. However, the final time, the one that actually resulted in me being taken to the hospital, there is a gap in time. I do not remember the attempt.

I should not be here today and it is only by the grace of God that I am able to share my testimony and breathe life and hope into others. My final attempt brought me to a hospital. How did I get there? A young man, that I dubbed my guardian angel, noticed something was wrong with me and would not leave me, even when I begged him to. Instead, he called for help. That act of selflessness is what opened my eyes and allowed me to see God's hand even when I felt I was so far away from him. That man listened to his instincts and allowed God to use him to not only save my life, but to start a ripple effect that is so profound.

Another pivotal moment was in the hospital. When I awoke the next morning I still had no answers, however the hospital said they would release me to the care of a responsible adult. My parents had left the hospital when they informed them I would be kept for observation. After the doctor reevaluated me in the morning he asked if I had anyone there. I did not know. They went out into the waiting room and there sat my mom. She had come back to get me…and that is when I realized that I was loved and there was more to life.

I cannot say that after that experience my life was perfect and everything fit together just right. Perhaps life got a bit messier for me because that next year I chose to drink my pain away. I did see a counselor, and I learned how to cope with life in a more productive way. I graduated college and a month before my graduation my grandfather died. It was another dark time for me, but I never thought about ending my life. I got a job; a friend of my grandfather's took me under his wing and I learned how to live life.

I have not only experienced multiple suicide attempts in my personal life, I have also been impacted by the loss of a loved one who completed suicide. Fast-forward four years. A month before my wedding I got a call that rocked my world to the core. That man that I looked up to, that filled the empty shoes of my grandfather in my life had decided he did not want to live anymore and used a gun to end it. That was the man that I was going to ask to walk me down the aisle. It hurt so bad, I never shared my testimony with him. I do not think he had any idea of my struggle with suicide and depression. I wish he would have reached out to me, so that I would have had the opportunity to share with him.

That is why this book is so important, it shares our stories in an effort to let the millions of others struggling with these thoughts know they are not alone. That experience of losing the man that I looked up to from suicide really opened my eyes. The hurt and pain I was feeling at the moment of that phone call and the days and months and years to follow, the unanswered questions, the 'what ifs;' all of that is still so real. At that moment, I realized what I would have done to my family and friends if God hadn't saved me from every suicide attempt.

Today, God has brought me so far. He has given me an amazing husband, more than I could have ever asked for. He has blessed us with two children that complete our family. He has given us life and more abundantly, contentment, peace, love; all of the things that I never thought were for me. I have a career that is continuing to grow and flourish with every step I take in faith. He has all of that for you too, but you have to believe and hold on a little longer.

When dealing with depression, one thing to know is that it is a mindset that most often the person does not have control over. As a child or young adult you cannot even begin to find the words to convey your feelings and what is happening within you. It does not feel like a choice when you are living it. This is why thought patterns and empowerment of control over your thoughts is so important. This has been an important key in my recovery from depression. Retraining my brain to see the positives in life and knowing that God is a good father and is in control. His truths have helped me tremendously. I stay in the Bible and pray constantly. When I begin to stray away from the word and my relationship with Jesus, my mind slips back into its old ways. I have learned to take my thoughts captive and speak truth over them. It does not mean that the thoughts do not come; it is more of how I deal with them now.

Music has been another large part of my recovery journey. It has always been a staple in my life. I finally surrendered my music over to God in 2010. I now listen to Christian music all of the time. It helps me to lift my spirit and keep me focused on the ultimate goal – loving Jesus because he loved me first. I have noticed if I turn the radio over to an old main stream song that I used to listen to, my attitude and thinking completely reverts back to my old ways. When I change it back to contemporary Christian music I feel the change again. It is odd but music does that to me and it may do that to one of you reading this book. Give it a try and see how you feel.

Please do not look down on a person who is struggling with thoughts of suicide or depression. They are in a dark place where they need love and hope spoken to them. We are to lift one another up and encourage each other. They may not want the help, but the help you give today may be what turns their life around, and they will never know how to thank you for your compassion and love at that very moment that could save their life. Your impact could be so widespread just by saving one person's life. The person that loved me and would not leave me right before I was taken to the hospital not only saved me, but also all of my generations to come. He saved the heartache of my family and friends. Everyone that I impact in my life today is a direct result of that young man's choice to not listen to me, rather he understood that I needed help, and for that I am eternally grateful.

My faith has taught me that I am a child of God and I know that he is in control. I am not to play God anymore by trying to end my life; he knows when it is my time and I will trust his good and perfect plan for my life. I am to bring my cares and burdens, lay them at the feet of his throne, and he will take care of them for me. He may not take care of them the way I think he should, but I know that he is a good and loving father and because of that I trust him no matter what the answer may look like.

Chapter 3

Flying the Soul Back Home

by Jenni Eden

I can't believe where I am now, compared to how I was so many years ago. I would never have imagined back in my youth that I would feel so grounded, assured, confident and happy. I have learnt some amazing strategies along my many years of struggling with depression, and I now use everything I have learnt to help others. I call it planting positivity.

For the purpose of helping others I now write about my blackness, with the only intention of helping shed some light on what is a dark, horrid, insular, frightening and isolating time. I remember how I felt and I remember one particular night so vividly that it seems like yesterday, even though it was actually 30 years ago this year (2016). It was the night I thought my life would end and in many ways it did, because after this night everything changed for me. So here is my story.

At the time of the story (1985), my parents were really struggling with their relationship; they had done for around 10 years. Home life was very stressful, emotional, and aggressive; it was frightening at times. It was painful and as it became more painful and upsetting to be in the family home, I began to see an escape route with my boyfriend even though I was only sixteen. I began to dream of a future with my boyfriend, of him taking me away from the madness of home.

But unfortunately it was not to be, my boyfriend went away to college where he found someone else, so, just when I needed rescuing the most, he left.

I was devastated. Everything inside of me was crumbling; it was like an internal avalanche, everything cascading down into the depths. The outside of me remained, but the inside was a mess, my thoughts, my emotions were plummeting and swirling. I felt like I was swirling in a vat of black tar unable to get out.

I felt so unhappy that I found it difficult to face each day. I didn't see a future now and my past, and my family was dissolving around me. I tried but all I could do was drag myself around feeling heavy, so heavy with despair. I felt that my unhappiness was like a black cloud, like gauze, covering everything. I felt everyone I was in touch with became tainted with my utter despair and gloom. I felt I was dragging people down.

I felt such pain inside, I felt so disjointed, that sometimes I would try to cut myself, thinking it would help me release all of the pain that was inside. I felt that inside of me was this toxic poison and if I could bleed it out, the poison would go away and I might be able to feel better.

I felt weak, I felt pathetic, and I was vulnerable. I was bitterly unhappy because I knew I was making others unhappy too and so I felt a huge guilt and huge shame. I couldn't help myself to feel better.

I felt responsible for dragging people down. Some friends tried to reach out to me, but I could not receive anything from them. I just felt that as I swirled slowly in this thick vat of treacle that I was bringing them into it with me and so the best thing was to not have connections, so that I could not make them suffer like I was suffering.

I can't begin to describe the overwhelming feeling of sadness. I had been rejected by my mother, through most of my childhood, it felt like, but now I was rejected by someone who I had felt such love for and who I had felt, loved me so much. I had felt accepted and so the rejection felt even harsher.

Where did it go wrong? Why did it go wrong? How was I supposed to carry on?

I had nothing to offer anyone, I had nothing to give to anyone, all I seemed to do was take away happiness, and takeaway joy, but I couldn't take away my pain.

I can't begin to tell you how deeply the sorrow flooded me. But I really couldn't see any other way. I felt suicide was the only answer.

I needed some courage in order to carry out what needed to be done. I felt I needed to pull myself together and so I went up to my room. I got into bed and tucked myself under the duvet to compose myself. I was going to give myself some crying time and then I was going to give myself a stiff talking to and then, I was going to end my life. It really did seem the best thing for me to do and it seemed best for everyone around me.

There was nothing for me to live for.

Whilst I was crying underneath my duvet there seemed to be warmth and brightness in the room. At first I thought it was the central heating.

This awareness of warmth seemed to seep into my conscious. I poked my head out of the duvet and saw that the light was not on; I saw that the curtains were closed too and so it was not the streetlight beaming through either, but what I did see was a small ball of light, it was like the size of a tennis ball. It was hazy, shimmering; it was bright white with hints of blue in it.

I pulled myself back under the duvet. I wanted to get on with the feeling sorry for myself, I wanted to carry on with the sobbing, I wanted to moan about my life, my existence, how unfair everything was, how cruel everything was, how worthless I was. I was raging inside my mind, mentally drawing the pictures of my tragedy and pain, constantly putting in my 'woe is me,' making sure I felt bad, bad enough to end it. But a small part of my mind was now curious, was that a ball of light I saw?

So once again I pulled back the duvet to look in the direction of where the tennis ball sized beam of light was. It was no longer there, instead in its place was a ball of light the size of a beach ball, the ball of light had grown and I could feel its warmth, so I could feel it reaching towards me.

I had no idea what it was and by now I was a little frightened. And that's when I felt the ball of light, as it sat on my bed.

There was actual weight to this light because it sat on my foot. I thought to myself, *Oh great, I'm going mad, and I am being squashed too.* Then a voice that seemed to be inside my head said *sorry* and the weight that was sitting on my foot moved over, towards the end of the bed and off my foot.

I was stunned into physical and mental silence.

And then this light spoke to me.

I can't remember everything exactly but it said something like, "Jenni you are deeply loved, you are loved unconditionally, you cannot leave until you have done all you need to do and there is much to do."

I did not know what to think I did not know what to say. What I did know was that I was no longer crying and that I no longer felt bad. I let the words seep in. As the words flooded my conscience the tears dried up. I could not seem to think of a reason to feel quite so bad. In fact, when I checked in with myself, I actually felt vibrant, happy, excited even and alive. I needed somehow to capture the experience. I removed the duvet to ask some questions but the light had gone. I felt creative and being an artist I had rolls of paper and ink in my room, so I began painting out black ink dancers, leaping in a celebratory, triumphant, energetic way.

This was such an incredible experience, for me it really was life changing and even though this was December 1986, I remember it so vividly, I remember the feeling so powerfully!

I began to wonder if this thing had been God. The light had now disappeared from my room. I opened the window and spoke to the sky. I said, "If you are God, I won't go to church, but I will meet you in gardens to talk."

Since that day I have constantly been in touch with this source of energy it has inspired many paintings, I have grown and I have learnt so much. Where ever I live, I create a garden to rest and connect in. My first love did come back in 1987, we married in 1994 and we've been together ever since. I knew something incredible had saved me and the only name I could really give it was God.

I still struggled with depression and at times it was manic and very severe but I knew deep down I really was loved and I knew deep down that I was enough. I knew that I mattered; I made a difference to this universe, somehow.

Chapter 4

Freedom

by Joy Kolodziejczyk

I grew up in Michigan and then lived in Chicago for a number of years. Four years ago I moved to my heaven on earth, Wisconsin. It was exactly what I needed to start over.

I am bipolar, I was diagnosed when I was 19. I'm 40 now and it's been a constant battle. Even before I was diagnosed I went 20 plus years feeling suicidal. Now I feel better, I can consider myself well. I'm not 'normal' but I am well enough that I don't have suicide on my mind every second of the day.

I've always told people about my suicide ideation and attempt. It's something I'm really close to. Because of iRise it just seems like a natural fit to tell my story. I'm nervous, I'm scared, I kinda don't want to tell my story but at the same time I do because it's the right thing to do, it could change someone's life.

I don't think people know how severe bipolar disorder can be; I've wanted raise awareness of what people in my situation go through. It absolutely effects all areas of your life.

I was 15 when I first noticed changes in my moods. I had a miserable kind of upbringing, so you never could tell what was causing what. But there was really no access to help. I think my mom threw me into a therapist for a little while because I wouldn't obey her when I believed she was incorrect. That really backfired and it was the last I saw of therapy for another 15 years.

I was always on my own; I was always alone, *always*. I never had anybody to go to. I was messing around with medications and stuff when I was in my teens. It wasn't enough to kill me but I didn't know that. Each time I thought I would die, but I didn't. It was just nuts.

The most serious occurrence had a lot to do with my mom and what was going on in the family. The demands that had been placed on me my whole childhood and taking care of her. My bipolar couldn't handle that. People were putting me under too much stress and I was saying so but no one would listen or leave me alone.

So I started drinking pretty heavily; I just wanted to relax. My prescribed dose was 4-5 pills. This would have allowed me to relax, to chill for a bit. I took 8. I looked at them in my hand and knew they were too many but I took them anyway. I don't know like if it's the 'grey area' of suicide but I'd say it's more suicide than not.

The hospital thought it was suicide because I had to go in; I almost died. Let me tell you something, when you almost die and you see the doctor shaking his head, saying he hopes you'll be ok but isn't sure, you do not want to die, you don't. Whatever you have on your mind, whatever you *think* you want to do...you *don't*. You *don't* want that. After this I attempted to get better but it took me another few years to get out of Michigan and to get up here and where I can live a peaceful free life.

Depression, I think that it's a full body problem. It's mental, it's emotional and it's physical. People who are like me just can't get out of bed, they really can't. It's like being in pain, you hurt everywhere. And mentally, everything is so overwhelming. Just trying to make a cup of coffee is impossible and then emotionally you are depressed, I was all over the board, experiencing too many emotions at one time. I couldn't sort them out. I had therapy for a long time, and I'm still having it. That and medication makes a huge difference. It keeps me healthy.

The last three doctors that I've had have been really, really good. The ones before that, I don't think they knew what they were doing. That's another challenge. When you are not doing well, trying to screen for a good therapist- you're totally incapable. People really need help making contact with a qualified therapist/doctor. Therapy and medication. Both were equal. I mean, I did show up and try and worked through a lot of pain. At the time I felt I didn't have much support outside of that. So I'm not gonna include anyone in that. Now I do. Now I have support.

On February 1st, 2012, I felt I could finally breathe again when I got in the truck and started driving up to Wisconsin, by myself with a big old truck and a cat. That was freedom! I celebrate that day like it's Christmas. I love that day. The day I felt free from it all and could live a normal life. It wasn't too late for me 'cause I was 36 at the time. I wasn't 100 when I made the decision. I wanted to start over so that's what I did.

I don't claim to know how to help someone with suicidal thoughts. I am not equipped to do that so I usually offer the suicide helpline number. However, what helped me was knowing my mind was lying to me, it played tricks on me, it was not 'real.' Your feelings are real but the act of actually doing it, it's your mind playing a dirty trick on you and you shouldn't listen to it. Knowing that really helped me.

To the person who is suicidal I say to them: get help. There's good help out there for those who are suffering. I know there is. Even though it seems like it's hopeless now, life is a gift and you really need to try it again tomorrow. 'Cause you don't know what tomorrow is going to bring and if you end your life you are never going to know what you're gonna miss out on, what could change. You know it's a temporary state even though it does not feel temporary. I understand that, I did 20 years of that. But that was what I was trying to convince of myself through that whole time was maybe it's just temporary, maybe it will go away. This day wasn't too bad, you know, I just view it as a temporary state.

I do believe that it is so powerful when people are able to wrap their head around the fact that it's a temporary thing. Feelings come and go; those feelings of despair and just being at the bottom will end.

It's a cliché but I feel like if you're at the bottom you can only go up. And you will. I think people need help, I don't think I could have tackled this by myself, I needed help.

To people who have not struggled with depression or suicide: educate yourself, take 5 minutes and read something. You can't play it off. Don't ever tease someone. Treat it seriously, very seriously, as if they had high blood pressure. Remember, this could be you someday. Engage them, talk to them. Try to find out what's going on and if you're not comfortable get them an appropriate phone number and say "Here you really should call here I'm worried about you." At least do that.

The biggest thing in my life now is freedom, having my freedom, maintaining my freedom and feeling peaceful. I found this inspirational quote by Jean-Paul Sartre yesterday. It says, "Freedom is what you do with what's been done to you."

Chapter 5

Suicide Solution

by Jami Keller

When I was 13 my parents went to Las Vegas for spring break. They left me home with my brothers in the care of my mom's parents for nine days. Grandma Daisy and Grandpa Tom gave me free range and watched my brothers. I had recently received some weights from my uncle Johnny, and decided to build myself a bench press out of some wood I found in the garage.

The week had gone beautifully. I went to my first Community Center dance, and was enjoying lifting weights in my bedroom. The day that my parents were due back home, my grandparents departed early, and there were a few hours of waiting for my parents to arrive. When they got home, my mom came in and promptly announced that they were going out to dinner without us, leaving my brothers and me home alone again. I was excited to show my dad my new bench press.

Dad came in and was in a hurry. He greeted me, and the next second he flew into a rage, yelling with full force as he grabbed the bench I had made and threw it into the garage, smashing it to pieces. At the top of his lungs he yelled at me, his face full of red-purple rage, "Never touch my tools and lumber again!"

They immediately walked out the door and left me to babysit my brothers.

It was crushing to the point of feeling completely numb. Transitioning from the freedom of not having him home for the week, to this sudden reminder of how completely fucked up my life was in his presence was unbearable.

As the numbness subsided, I felt totally hopeless. I could not take it any longer. I was done. My brothers had retreated to their shared room. I walked to the kitchen and found the bottle of aspirin. It was a medium sized white plastic bottle with just enough pills to cover the bottom of the container. I poured them into my mouth and drank them down.

Relief washed through my body. It was over. I went and lay down on my bed. I let everything go. There was a detachment that allowed thoughts to flow through my head without judgment. I could no longer be responsible for taking care of my parents. Their dysfunction was no longer mine to deal with; I would no longer be here. That included my brothers who I loved dearly, and while Steven would receive more of the brunt of my dad's anger with me out of the picture, I could not protect him from it, at least not any longer. It was done.

The only sadness I felt was for my friend Tom. We were best friends, and he deserved a good-bye. I picked up the phone and called him. I told him that we would not be hanging out, and that I really appreciated his friendship. He asked me why and I told him what I had just done. Before I could finish my explanation he was at my door in his socks with tears angrily streaming down his face. "What the fuck are you doing, man?" he cried.

His parents were right behind him. His dad took me to the emergency room, where they gave me ipecac. I expulsed the contents of my stomach, and it felt like it was all the way from the tips of my toes.

My parents arrived. My mom came in first to my hospital room. "What were you thinking?" she asked.

I told her I just couldn't take it anymore. Then my dad walked in. He was pissed but showing a calm demeanor to everyone watching. He would not look at me, and looking at Mom he gave her a face of frustration and what I knew was anger because I had embarrassed him, and the family name. That was a bad sign.

They took me home, and there was a counseling appointment about two weeks later. When the day finally arrived I was too numb to even say anything, and there were no more counseling visits.

I began self-medicating with alcohol and marijuana, oh and girls. Those things kept me from suicide for the years of living with my parents; the relief and the 'fun' I could engage in by checking out, dissociating, seemed to make life worth it.

It took me another seventeen years to get to the place of understanding that I was passively suicidal. The tools we teach people now are all inspired because so many people end up feeling this way, trauma or not.

What everyone needs to know is that it is *all fixable*! The skills to heal are not even all that difficult, they just have to be done!

Jami Keller's book *Passively Suicidal No More* is available at PassionProvokers.com or Amazon.com

Chapter 6

There's Always Another Way

by Keith Blakemore-Noble

I had all the equipment I needed, all ready for the act.

I had tested that everything worked correctly, there'd be no embarrassing mistakes, no risk of it not working completely.

All I needed was the date. This needed a little careful planning so as to minimise distress to others. I had a theatrical commitment to honour, then there were a couple of family birthdays - no sense in marring those forevermore - and so the date was set for 3 weeks in the future.

Finally, this time, nothing would go wrong. Finally, this time, I would at long last be freed from this miserable, unbearable, hopeless despair of an existence.

Third time lucky, one might put it.

The first time was when I was in my final year at university. I would have been 21 years old, in a deep depression (not that I realized this at the time), and things had been so utterly bleak for me for so long that one night I had enough. I could see no way out. There was no alternative. I swallowed all the paracetamol I had, and washed them down with some vodka, lay down on my bed, and went to sleep, feeling relieved that I would never wake up again…and then feeling really annoyed when I woke up again the next morning!

(Thinking about it, I assume I was just very lucky and had not taken nearly enough to be fatal, nor, thankfully, enough to cause long term damage.)

Looking on the bright side though, I was less depressed, some of those feelings of depression had made way for anger at failing to kill myself, which lead to curiosity about what went wrong. Of course, that curiosity was not able to contain itself, and spilled over into curiosity about how else I could handle things instead.

It was only a little spark, but even the smallest of sparks can, under the right circumstances, start a fire. Sure enough, that spark caused me to reconsider things, and I found another way to get through things and I actually started looking to the future with some level of anticipation for the first time in a long while.

Seems there was another way after all.

Fast forward about 4 years and we find the second time. The depression had returned, with a vengeance. Same sort of causes as before, and now coupled with a very deep sense of utter despair at being perpetually single - by this time it seemed that all of my friends and acquaintances were wither getting married, in long-term relationships, or happily jumping from one-nighter to one-nighter.

And me? Completely, totally and perpetually single, never even a hint of interest from anyone, totally unable to figure out how to change that, and facing a lifetime of increasingly crushing loneliness. So that night I decided that as pills had not worked last time, this time I would try good old wrist-slashing.

I learned that this method would be painful, so I decided to enlist the help of good old alcohol to help me numb the pain (both physical and mental). Naturally, this meant I ended up drinking quite a lot, and I passed out, waking up the next morning with a sore head, sore and itchy cuts on my wrists, but of course none got deep enough.

So now I had to not only continue to face life, somehow, but also to keep my wrists hidden for a while.

But something interesting happened. I got to talking about what had happened with someone and before I knew it, we were meeting up regularly for tea and a chat…

There's always another way.

So, here we are. February 2013. A good few years since the second time, a few failed relationships under the bridge (if one may be permitted to mix one's metaphors).

Single (again - dumped every time, never saw it coming each time); unemployed (redundancy the previous year); deeply in debt; a few weeks from being completely broke; no future, nothing to live for, no way out. The mortgage company would repossess once I defaulted, goodness knows what the other loan companies would do (the perils of financing when in a good job, then finding that job disappearing unexpectedly). I felt like I had nothing to live for.

I had all the equipment I needed. I had tested that everything worked correctly. I had settled on the date. I could have found a way to bear the remaining 3 weeks a little more easily knowing that the end was in sight.

Then something happened. Someone reached out to me and asked for help.

Help which would require me selling up everything and moving for a period to the other side of the world (namely Bali).

The curious thing is, this person had suggested the same course of action 6 months earlier, but I felt I was not able to help - there was no way I could sell everything and up-sticks to the other side of the world. And yet here they were, making the same suggestion 6 months later.

What did I do?

I phoned the estate agent the next morning, put my house on the market, sold up, and moved to Bali (originally for 3 months, I ended up staying there for 18).

Curious! Exactly the same suggestion; first time it was not within my realms of possibility, the second time it was literally a life-saver.

There *is* always another way!

Since then I've had another couple of bouts of depression, but this most recent time a friend talked me into seeing the doctor, who offered me pills which have been a great help. I know it is still there, lurking, but I am far better able to deal with it and to cope.

I still have bad days, still occasionally have those thoughts, but now I know they will only last fleetingly, and I am able to live a good life.

The depression is there, and it is under *my* control, not the other way round.

I definitely prefer this other way!

I've looked into things quite a bit this last year. Turns out that both my mother and her father suffered from life-long depression too. He ended his own life, my Mum came close at times. I discussed this with my doctor who confirmed that it is believed that there can be a genetic component to depression in some cases.

So now I accept that I am genetically predisposed to depression.

Which, in a weird way, actually helps me - I now know it's not something I'm doing wrong; it's not my failure to handle my mindset; it's just a part of who I am (asthma, myopia, depression).

And it is manageable with mild antidepressants. Just as my asthma is kept under control with my inhaler, and my vision is adjusted by my glasses.

I wish I'd known this way back before the first time. Looking back, I can see definite patterns and periods of depression running through my life. And I now realize that had I been in a position to seek medical advice, I would quite possibly have received the help I needed to be able to cope, and I would not have made those attempts on my life.

There is another way. I don't have to be depressed.

For some people, diet works. For others, meditation or religious faith seems to do the trick. For yet others, various psychological therapies help them to keep their depression under control. And for yet others, me included, medication seems to offer the key to unlocking the cage and allowing us to experience the freedom to, dare I say it, actually enjoy life.

Provided we recognise that we need help, and we are able to seek it.

One does *not* have to remain at the mercy of depression. One does not have to despair of life itself.

There is always another way.

No matter how hopeless one's situation may be, no matter what other options one has tried (diet, medication and physiological devices all failed to help me, for example), there is always another way.

The more people are able to open up and share their experiences, the more we can challenge the terrible stigma which still surrounds mental health, the more we will be able to help other people who are suffering without hope, to realize the reality.

No matter how hopeless it may seem.

No matter how useless one may feel.

There is always another way.

http://blakemore-noble.com

Chapter 7

Where Faith Begins

by Carrie

My name is Carrie; I am a single mom of three amazing kids and one beautiful granddaughter. I work in the mortgage industry and pride myself on being very professional. I am a religious person. I have a lot of faith in God because without him I wouldn't be here right now. So that is a little about me.

I decided to share my story after hearing my best friend share that her teenage daughter's friend committed suicide. My kids carry a lot of weight over what happened to me even though it was not their fault. It is never someone else's fault and I feel it is important for people to understand what a person is thinking when they do go through it and how it affects them. If I am able to stop one person from committing suicide then what I am doing is worthwhile.

I have always struggled with depression. My family always labeled me the emotional one, the cry baby, the doormat. I always struggled a lot with my parents' divorce and thought it was somehow my fault. I know now that was not true and it is not the child's fault. I have amazing parents but the back and forth and watching them argue was difficult. I told I was an attention seeker but really I just didn't know how to deal with what I felt.

I hid my depression well for many years till after my divorce. I just kind of struggled with it throughout the years chalking it up to life. I lived a very quiet life through my marriage. It was more of a Suzie homemaker type, always trying to be the perfect wife. Stifling my feelings to not create issues.

Things changed after my divorce. I didn't know who I was anymore. I spent 20 years being someone's wife and mother. I really was completely lost. When my husband cheated on me I felt like there was something wrong with me. I focused on trying to lose weight, stop eating, trying to fix the things that I felt that caused my marriage to end. When I found out he was cheating I blamed myself and then started having thoughts of harming myself. I know this is terrible to say but I would have rather found out he died than he cheated because at that point it made me deficient. I was separated from my husband. I was going through marriage counseling, by myself, funny enough. I relied on the church to help me.

After so many hours of counseling he still cheated. He was not interested on fixing our marriage. After nine months apart he decided one day he wanted to come home. Three days later he changed his mind. I was so sad and so I went out one night and met someone who I considered the love of my life. I fell hard for him. I relied heavily on my church at that time because they were my saving grace. They supported me through my separation but then something changed. The person I trusted at church with my situation started to tell me I was an adulterer for loving this man while my divorce was not final. This cut me to my core. I did not leave my family; why was I accused of doing what my husband did? I stopped going to church. That was my safe place and now I had none.

Fast forward a year and I am now going through a divorce, bankruptcy and about to lose the man of my dreams. One morning out of the blue he said he couldn't do it anymore and he broke up with me. That was the icing on top of the cake. I was crushed and I remember going into automatic. I wasn't feeling. I didn't want to feel. I went and kissed my kids' goodbye like any ordinary morning. I knew exactly what I was doing and didn't think beyond ending the pain. I drank a bottle of wine and overdosed on over 150 pills. I should not have survived. My little girl found me. I have no memories of that time. The only recollection is through my kids.

They saw what no children should ever have to see. The police officer hitting my face and shaking me; I was unresponsive. My oldest in the Emergency Room watching them work on me. I woke up three days later seeing my mother's devastated face and my three kids staring down at me.

My youngest daughter was completely and utterly devastated. Not only was she dealing with my attempt but three years earlier her grandfather committed suicide. She felt like she couldn't depend on anyone because they would be gone. Every time I didn't answer the phone she would go into utter panic thinking I was gone. I have to live with that for the rest of my life. I will never forgive myself for that. I never wanted to hurt my kids, that is something I never wanted to do. People say suicide attempts are selfish. You don't go into it being selfish. You can't think. All you want is to end the pain and make it stop. You want to stop hurting and hurting everyone else. This is so difficult to share. I'm crying as a write this.

The signs were there but I didn't see them. I was quiet and isolated myself. I felt myself getting more and more depressed by the day and having negative thoughts. I wish I would have known the signs. I have learned not to allow myself to become isolated because it is one of my triggers. I had placed myself in the hospital once when I felt my depression getting worse after my attempt. I have learned to deal with my illness and seek help when I need it. When asked how I am able to overcome suicidal thoughts, I have to say every time I look into my kids' faces I see what I've done. What I can never do again. I did go through extensive counseling and hospitalization when it happened. I can recognize the triggers now. I also renewed my faith in God and started attending church again. My pastor came to visit me in the hospital and his presence was profound. He told me how worthwhile I was and how God isn't finished with me yet. I still struggle everyday but you know what? I'm gonna make it because God intends me to be here. I have a higher purpose, whether it's to share my story or whether it's to just love my family; that is why I am here. I will never stop trying and will always be here for anyone else who is struggling. This is an illness and awareness brings hope. If I can save one person from doing what my father-in-law did or what I attempted to do, then my job is complete. We are not alone.

Chapter 8

Flipping the Switch on Passive Suicide
by Donna Davis

The sadness finds us all from time to time. We are no strangers to the constant borage of media coverage of horrible events, natural disasters, wars all over the world and bullying, bickering and judgement no matter which way you turn. It's usually a little closer to home as it involves us or people that we know.

Most times we can handle it, sometimes it overwhelms us and we can't seem to get away from it. If left to its own devises the misery can drag us down into the depths of despair and anguish with seemingly no end in sight as it holds us in its death grip.

Which end is up? Is there an end to all this pain and agony? Unfortunately, many think that ending their lives is the only way to make it stop – or go away. I can certainly understand these feelings.

Unfortunately, this doesn't solve the problems and we may leave behind so many who really would miss us. We can compound their pain by our permanent absence whether we know it or not, whether we believe it or not, and the cycle continues.

Our distress clouds our vision and understanding; we can contemplate suicide just to make all the overwhelming heaviness stop! At times there doesn't seem to be any other choice. We try to numb ourselves out with different things but sometimes it just doesn't work.

My dilemma came at an early age. I didn't believe in suicide. My belief was that I did not create myself so I had no right to destroy myself. I couldn't bear to disappoint my creator. For some reason, unbeknownst to me, I was put here for a purpose, and I did not want to mess that up. Unfortunately, I was distracted by all my sorrow and barely had a 'life.' I went from day to day, plodding along with barely any direction or real care about a bright future or happy life- that seemed to be for other people, not me. Somehow others found happiness and it seemed to be fleeting for me. A little here, a little there, but it never seemed to last long. The next event or tragedy wasn't far away. It seemed endless, hopeless.

Since I couldn't take my life I lived a life of desperation and sorrow. Mending pieces here and there and pretending everything was 'ok.' I did pretty well at pretending and often no one knew how very sad and lonely I was. I was a high functioning depressed person most of my life. I wore many masks that seem to hide my true feelings and/or deflect inquiry. I rode this roller coaster for many decades.

There are years of disturbing memories, months of tragedy, weeks of 'shut down' or 'breakdown,' days that were hard to even get out of bed, hours spent reminiscing about 'if only,' minutes constantly ticking away, unlived.

This led me to realize that I wasn't actively participating in suicide but I sure was doing it passively. I was becoming aware that apathy, drama and silence seemed to control my life. I became cynical and sarcastic - caught in confusion and didn't know which direction to turn.

Little by little I found the courage to change my life around.

Instead of destroying myself I set out to destroy the pain. I was open to almost all possibilities for improvement even though they seemed so out of reach at the time.

As I gathered more knowledge and information I came up with creative ideas and found ways to cope, to push through and sometimes even thrive. With more and more success I was able to flip the switch on the depression and make a conscious decision to live fully and happily as often as I could.

My main motto became "This too shall pass." I would repeat this to myself somehow knowing that nothing lasts forever, and that includes misery. Somewhere there was light at the end of the tunnel and I was focusing on that! I didn't always see it but I *knew* it was out there somewhere. I talked myself into believing it because I was just so tired of wanting giving up.

I would also find a point of interest - something to think about and have right in front of me, so to speak, that would take up my time and attention instead of all the dread…sort of like prompting a horse by putting a carrot out in front of it. I found that sooner or later I *would* get to my goal and that would make me smile, feel accomplished and *prove* to myself that I *could* change the tide.

I would question how could one person have so much trauma and tragedy in their life (referring to myself) and so many others were living a life of nirvana?

Most of my misery came from wishing it were different, wanting to change the past or control the future…all are virtually futile. Instead I learned that I can aim for things and head towards them.

Yes, there are roadblocks and minefields full of triggers and memories that seem to rub salt in my wounds. I would keep singing and repeating "Let It Be" as a private prayer to help me stay on the right path.

I took the chance to open up to the world around me, little by little and see what was possible. What could be different? What was I willing to look at differently? What could I forgive? What could I heal? What could I let go of in order to have a better life?

One day I came across an Oprah clip. It talked about how we get caught in the cycle of feeling sorry for ourselves, etc. She suggested that instead of getting lost in a constant litany of woes that have us circling back into our old patterns, that we only allow ourselves 5 minutes for a pity party. At first I thought she was crazy because of course I could go on for hours and days and here she was saying – no- just 5 minutes. So I took her up on her advice and was amazed at how much more time I now had for looking forward to a better solution rather than wallowing in the cesspool of my past thoughts. It worked and I was hooked! It took some practice. Things that had plagued me for years were put on notice that things were going to be different now. I was in charge of my changes and I was going to make it matter!

Instead of focusing solely on suffering, I would seek out information of others, of survivors. To study and learn that there *are* possibilities for help, kindness, healing and thriving. It's *never* too late.

And in the words of Maya Angelou (from an interview), "I was able to draw from human thought, human disappointments, and triumphs, enough to triumph myself."

When I realized that I could make a choice (other than giving up) there was a world of possibility both now and in my future-should I decide and accept those possibilities. I wasn't alone. I wasn't the only one who ever felt this way. There *was* a way to make it better!

I had to change my mindset and find other like-minded people who had experiences equal or worse than my own. I tuned into their will, their survival, their courage and strength and made them my own.

It was then that I found a way to take the 'charge' off my emotions with a process called 'tapping' and it allowed me to release old patterns, stored up toxic emotions and pain.

When I didn't know how I would do it or where to turn I would find solace, comfort and encouragement from people who I had never met, nor ever would. They helped me climb out of my anguish and to give each day another chance to show me just how good life could be, even if at the beginning it was 'just better than yesterday.' I started adding up the possibilities and found that I too could heal and move on. Do I slip back from time to time? Sure. But now I am more consciously aware of my options, reactions and behavior- which influences my outcome in a much healthier, happier, hopeful way. Instead of being down and out I can look up and believe in better days.

It's never too late to look for a rainbow. At first someone else might show you one or become one for you. Before you know it, you become one yourself and when you do, you turn around and brighten someone else's day as they make their way to becoming their own rainbow.

It's *your* turn.

Chapter 9

The Sinister Secret that Almost Destroyed Me
by Marcia Diamond

Secrecy was a common thread that wrapped me in a personal silence for most of my childhood. My family had secrets and to talk about them, was tantamount to being a traitor during war. My father was a functioning alcoholic – which brought its own set of 'secret' rules and behaviors. A baby out of wedlock, suicide, bigotry, divorce, ex-communication...so many secrets.

But, there was *one*– a secret so big, so emotional, that when I uncovered this 'thing' it felt like a bomb went off in my heart, and my family's code of *don't talk* sent ripples of betrayal planting more seeds of shame and guilt, changing my world forever.

I was 19, had finished high school, and during the 9 months leading to uncovering the secret, I used drugs, was involved in a felony drug bust, ran away to Texas with a man I didn't know, had affairs with several married men, including my attorney, lost a roommate to suicide and then began to contemplate my own demise. Poor choices and my promiscuous behavior left me without feelings of self-worth. Yet, I didn't know why or how to stop. The attention I did get fed the treadmill of self-worth enough, to keep me returning to it, and I hated myself every time.

One afternoon, I was wandering alone in a depressed stupor when I made a choice to get help and walked through the doors of a psychologist's office. After calming me down, the psychologist began to ask a series of questions to help establish a timeline and to gain an understanding of what troubled me. But when I couldn't recall chunks of time from my childhood, he asked if I was willing to try hypnotherapy. I had an inkling of what to expect since I had been hypnotized during a school event my college held the year before. Once I was under, he said he would guide my inner-child back in time, allowing me to experience my memories as that small child. It didn't take long for the therapist to induce a trance, allowing my body and mind to move into a state of complete relaxation. When my breathing steadied, the doctor asked me to recall my earliest memory.

During the session, I did relive the times that I had suppressed. It brought troubling memories of incest perpetrated by my grandfather and centered on religion with rewards of candy bars I otherwise was forbidden to eat. So many memories came flooding back that my emotions ran from shock to anger, and then guilt and shame. It was almost too much to process.

After being hypnotized and uncovering the truth about my grandfather's incestuous behavior and the years of sexual abuse to me and one other sister, I continued seeing the psychologist for several more sessions. Although I was gaining a better understanding of what happened to me and the psychological damage it caused, I was emotionally confused and scared because I knew what the next step was. When the therapist thought I was ready, I broke the vow of secrecy and told my mother.

Refusing to believe me, I was crushed under a giant bolder of my mother's betrayal. I tried again with my two older sisters only to be silenced by more rocks of denial. I was devastated by the rejection, and now it felt like I was bad, like I did something wrong. My shame core was filling up with more guilt.

For years, I lived with the shame and guilt that just maybe, I was crazy and that I did in fact conjure up this whole story. The man I married drank heavy and began doing drugs, mixed with my emotions, it was a volatile situation. Twice I ended up in the hospital from his blows, and once I was so depressed, I put a gun to my head. Thankfully, he slammed it away as I was pulling the trigger. (Even as I write this I feel a twinge of shame.)

I began going to Al-anon, to deal with his drinking and my depression. It was there, for the first time, I told my story. People I never met were compassionate and they believed me. I was encouraged to make peace with myself and with my grandfather by confronting him. I had to know if I was crazy or not. I had to know if my story was true, if I had been a victim of my grandfather's sickness and an ugly family secret. It gave me hope.

I penned a letter to my grandfather informing him of my young memories and what he did. To my relief, he responded in a letter, admitting to his incestuous behavior. After confessing, he asked me *not* to speak about our little secret to the rest of the family.

Now I had proof. I was not crazy. It was a *huge* relief, knowing that what I believed happened, did happen. I questioned whether or not 'prove' to my family that I was not a liar? More guilt and shame. I made the decision to keep the truth to myself. I was not willing to risk more rejection. After all, my grandfather's admission felt like a load of bricks off my shoulders. I could breathe again. I was going to be ok. I wasn't crazy.

At the age of 29, I really thought that uncovering the truth was all I needed – just to know the 'whys' of my behavior was my holy grail. Now I could live my life. But, in reality, I was far from being psychologically healthy. That same year, I divorced the man I was married to once I came to grips how our dysfunction and his drinking was adding to my mental instability. It was a classic case of me 'marrying my father the alcoholic' in order to fulfill my sick abandonment needs. Adding to life's stresses I changed jobs, bought a house and met my current husband.

But, my mental problems were not over. I wanted to believe I was handling life and the stresses that went along with it and no matter how hard I tried to 'whoosh' those negative and depressed feelings away, they plagued me even more. On this roller coaster of emotions, I had days I did not want to get out of bed, and had to force myself to go to work. I was constantly living on the emotional edge of chaos and desperate to find normal.

After several years, I finally decided to climb off of the emotional roller coaster I had learned to ride, and sought additional professional help.

During the first session with the psychologist, I told my story; the story of my existence and the shroud of fog I lived under; the story of my family and all of our warts. She shared with me that being an adult child of an alcoholic has its own set of behaviors not to mention adding sexual abuse on top of it. In fact, often time the two are interrelated.

I never really considered the implications of growing up with an alcoholic parent. Up until now, my focus was on my grandfather's sexual abuse. After all, my father was not a stumbling-in-the-gutter alcoholic nor was he an abuser. He worked every day and provided for his family. But alcohol was always there – leaving him passed out in his chair every night. He was non-existent.

After several sessions, I was beginning to learn why I felt the way I did. Why I felt so different from everyone else. Why I always judged myself so harshly and why I took everything so seriously. I understood the cause of why I would over-react to situations I had no control over and my constant seeking of approval from those around me not to mention the difficulties I have had in maintaining healthy relationships. And while I was beginning to understand that these were learned behaviors because of my childhood and the trauma I experienced, I didn't know how to shake off these feelings I had of self-loathing and turn them into self-love.

My psychologist suggested I attend a weekend workshop for adults who had experienced a childhood with alcoholic parents (and incest) she was hosting in her home. A practicing Buddhist, she introduced meditation as a helpful practice. I really thought I had dealt with my abuse and felt that the 'child of an alcoholic' is what I was really there for since I had confronted my abuser who, by this time, had succumbed to death by old age. But what I wasn't prepared for was an exercise in rage she had us participate in to deal with our hidden anger and emotional pain – allowing a safe place to 'let it out'. And boy did I – to both my grandfather and my dad.

This was a huge turning point in my life. I was not my thoughts. I left that weekend workshop feeling on top-of-the-world. I stepped on to a path that began with processing my pain and hidden anger. Now, I was on the road to recovery. I still had a lot of work ahead of me and I looked forward to my self-awareness.

Chapter 10

Unafraid to be Weak

by Matthew LuPone

My name is Matthew LuPone and I am a recent graduate from Point Park University's Cinema Department. Currently I in work retail and am working on producing a web series called *Brace* that should be online soon, while also in pre-production for two more web series. I want to start with this information so that you everyone can see that no matter how bad things can get, they can get *so* much better. I am now living out my dreams!

What makes it so important to tell my story now is that I am finally growing into my own as an adult and I have always wanted to help others. I know that telling my story here can help me reach a wide audience, and that is very important, not only to me, but to all of you reading these chapters.

I have suffered from some level of anxiety and depression for years. My issues started when I was very young, with your typical family issues. My father and I didn't really have much of a relationship until very recently because we are worlds apart in our interests. He likes sports, fishing, building things and staying in all day; I like shopping, designing clothing, traveling and watching movies. It was always hard for us to forge a connection and that was always very tough for me and it was hard to know if he knew that.

I had other family issues that continue to this day. I have never gotten along with my uncle or his wife. They have always told me to be realistic and that dreaming isn't worth it. They tried to control my emotions and behavior to fit their ideals, even when my parents were in the room. They've always made me feel small and unappreciated. Every holiday I would leave feeling defeated and miserable, but I would be guilted into going back next year because it's 'family.' Here's my two-cents: blood makes you a relative. Loyalty makes you family.

I went from having family issues to being a teenager and in high school. My township is full of wealthy people who think they are just God's gift to men. That isn't necessarily different than any of your townships, but it really is its own little bubble of snobbish self-importance. I don't want to say that I've ever struggled with being 'gay' because I don't personally believe in labels. I'm a human just like everyone else. And then I fell in love with my best friend. That didn't turn out so well and it turned my whole life upside down. I lost a few friends in the fallout (friends I believed would be life-long, but they clearly didn't give a shit about me).

That is when my mood changed drastically. I had been in counseling for quite some time, but this made me fall into the darkest despair I had ever known. I felt as though I were drowning and couldn't come up for air. It wasn't because I had lost the person I was in love with, it was because I had lost the person who I believed to be my best friend. He was so cruel and heartless towards me once people began to talk about me having feelings for him. The feelings never mattered to me, I would always choose to keep a friend I care for over destroying something good due to feelings, but that wasn't a possibility in his mind. My heart was torn into so many fragments that I wasn't sure I could ever put it back together.

There were days I couldn't even pull myself out of bed. It got so bad that I wouldn't go to school and I would only go to work. I had to keep my mind off of it. I worked at a family-owned pet shop back then and a puppy came in one day, a little girl. All of the other puppies in her litter were adopted so quickly, but not her. I fell for her instantly. She was my saving grace. She became my best friend in the world.

Almost eight months after I got her was the night I attempted suicide. It was the cast party for the high school musical and it was held at my ex-friend's house. I was only invited because I was in the cast and it would be too much of a spectacle to not invite me. I hadn't really thought of killing myself before that night. But everything changed that evening.

He had asked all of the guys to spend the night together for one last hoorah before some of us graduated, but told everyone not to tell me. When I found out, I was shaken to the core. I knew he was angry, but to do this? I felt humiliated. One of my very best friends at the time had hidden it from me as well, just to fit in. He lied right to my face. I raced home and cried myself to sleep. But I barely slept. When I woke, I couldn't handle it, so I took a razor blade and slit my wrists. Not deeply enough, thank God. Once I saw what I had done and saw Cobie (my darling puppy) sitting there watching me, I called my dad and he raced to find me. That was the darkest time in my life.

I know that was long, but I feel it's important to share all of that so everyone can see how deep it all went. I felt utterly alone. I was humiliated by so many people I cared about. Thank god for that little dog though because without her, I never would have made it through.

There are so many deep feelings that race through your head when it gets that dark. The world literally goes black. My mind was full of rage, hurt, despair, and so many other feelings. It just didn't seem as though there was another way. I didn't know how I could go back to school and face them all. It was so very difficult.

The fall after I graduated high school, I went to college. I thought it would be so different, so much better. And it was in so many ways, but I had suffered PTSD after all of the events of high school and classes of any kind triggered me terribly. The first semester was terrible and I was advised to drop a class by a professor, so I did. It turned out that class was one of the very foundation of my department and I was set back an entire year. I was distraught and pissed.

I took the next semester off to work and grow and just be me. That helped so much. I went back the next semester and for the following four years I learned so much. In the midst of the great, my grandfather passed and that was a hard hit. He was my mother's rock and she is mine, so that rocked me. After that I got a second dog; a brother for Cobie, named Barney. He helped a lot, just like she always had. I realized who I was and who I wanted to be. I met amazing people; professors and friends. I thought my life was perfect, and then I lost Cobie. She had autoimmune hemolytic anemia, which basically meant her body was destroying her red blood cells. Having to make the decision to put her down and watching her body go limp in my arm almost did me in. I thought I might fall into that deep despair once again, but I didn't. I thought of the joy she was to me and Barney will forever be a reminder of her as well.

I am now on an amazing path to starting a career in film and television and I couldn't be happier. I miss Cobie every day, but I know she is always with me. What people need to know about suicide is that it isn't black or white; it just is. When you come to that decision it is because it seems like the only decision, but it's *not*. You have to lift your head up, remember the good things in your life, just like my beautiful Cobie, and move forward. That's what I can tell you. That is for everyone, those who do and have struggle (d) with it and those who don't/haven't. Find love and light where you can.

I'm not religious, but when I'm low or angry I think *God grant me the serenity to accept the things I cannot change, the courage to change the things I can and the wisdom to know the difference.*

Another saying is one I always said to Cobie. "And in that moment, I swear, we were infinite." Because she and I will always be together. Infinite. Love.

Chapter 11

Rescued by God's Divine Intervention

by Gewanda J. Parker

Two days ago I read a text that said, *Pray for my friends, their 15-year-old son just ended his life.* I was hurt. Those words, his age, his method, lingered in my heart and mind. I once knew the magnitude of that kind of pain. I was saved by a ringing telephone. Who knows why I was spared and this young lad wasn't. I pondered the possibilities he had, the interventions he could have chosen, maybe. He didn't have to die. I know it's difficult to believe at those critical moments that it's better to stay put on this side and find long term relief than to choose a temporary solution. Today, I'm happy to embrace the fact that I failed at my own suicide attempt.

The memory of one of many of my suicidal thoughts flooded the corridors of my mind and psyche. I stopped for more than thirty minutes to sit in silence, to pray for this family. I prayed for the mother who would not see her son alive again. As I looked at my daughter running around playing with her toys, I couldn't imagine the magnitude of a mother's hurt from losing her son. The thoughts she must have; thoughts like *Did I do something wrong* and of course *what could I have done differently* surely crossed her mind. I prayed for the father, his legacy lost. What must he feel? I prayed for the young man's friends. I wondered, how many of them knew, who didn't take it seriously, were any in denial or dismissed his cries for help. Or just the opposite, did he hide it so well that everyone was shocked. Did he hide his despair? How long? I thought of my good friend, who had also lost her son to suicide some seventeen years ago. She stills struggles and grieves deeply.

That text took me back to the day, I said these words: *I can't get it out of my mind, the thoughts the pain, the anguish the despair, the hopelessness, the feelings of just wanting to end it all. If only I could escape, if only I could just exit my existence and leave this place, this space, this world, the state of mind. I need help. No, I'll just end it all!*

I tried to take my life. Yet I was unsuccessful, now as I look back over my life, this was the first and only time I am ever so grateful that I actually failed at something. You see, failure to me was something that held me in bondage and made me feel less than a human. Those ferocious thoughts of my failures encapsulated my mind. I continuously calculated the areas in my life where I had indeed failed at something. I lived in the in a mask of my true reality. It wasn't all bad, but I brought on unrealistic expectations of myself and the direction of my life and how I wanted it to be. I was overcome with grief, shame, humiliation and embarrassment. I failed a class in college, I'd lost my crown as the college queen, and the millions of friends, what we now call followers, were no longer around, I had failed myself.

These were my visible failures to the world. Yet, as I surveyed my current failures at that time I really was still holding on to those losses so long ago. The relationship I was in had gone sour. I'd made such a mess of what I thought my future would be or look like. I'd let my standards down. I had settled for less than what I deemed to be the best in life. I didn't have anyone to turn to. My life was simply an island surrounded by sea of people. Yet no one could enter that secluded place of failure, frustration, and sadness. Oh such deep seeded sadness; the kind that makes breathing difficult and illusions reality. If only I could have fallen into the black hole that engulfed me. My only glimmer of hope and bright light was somewhere else, but definitely not on this earth so my only option was to say goodbye to this world. Finally, I had found a solution. I would end it all and find relief. During those minutes I had no consciousness of anyone else, the opinions and feelings of others, at that point were mute in my head and heart. Life had no purpose. My plan started and I prepared to execute.

The easiest way was to drown pills, but they were only aspirin and not nearly enough to take me out. Cutting and missing the wrong vein would be too painful. So I decided to buy a bunch of different pills. Just as I prepared to walk out the door the phone rang. I hesitated. I waited. They called again and again. I answered. On the other line was a close friend who said, "God put you on my mind and heart this morning, just a quick call to check in on and let you know you matter to me and you are an amazing woman."

It must have been the gasp, or my disorientation, floodgate of tears but all I remember him saying is "Get out the house and go to the nearest church." I didn't understand much of what was going on at that moment except I was a puppet responding to the puppeteer. I followed his instructions, and got out the house. I got into my car and took off. He repeatedly said, "Keep driving!" I ran a red light. "Keep driving." I turned in front of a car.

"Keep driving, but stay on the phone."

I was so out of it I hadn't the foggiest clue of where I was headed, I just drove. The sight of a grocery store snapped me back into my plan of action and I parked to go in to buy bottles of different pills. He refused to hang up the phone with me.

We talked for what seemed like hours, with me in and out of sobbing, anger, disorientation. He kept saying, "If only you could find a church somewhere but just stay where you are until I can arrange someone to get you."

During our conversation, I looked up to see a sign. I had parked literally in front of a store-front church adjacent to the grocery. My friend convinced me to go inside. I did. When I walked in the preacher took one look at me, stopped her message, asked the congregation to join her in prayer because I needed God to save my life. They prayed, and the saving power of God intervened in my life that day, changed me and I have never looked back.

Since that time I'm constantly reminded of how blessed I am to be on this side. Had I gone through with taking my own life, I would not have been able to go ahead and become a mouth piece for those who are suffering with suicidal thoughts and attempts. I do not know another person's degree of pain, but I do know pain. The joy of living a fulfilled life today outweighs the misery I lived in my yesterdays.

Today I am the happiest mother to a darling little toddler. I pastor a wonderful congregation filled with love and true community. I wrote part one of my autobiography, which speaks to the pain and dysfunction I suffered in my childhood. The book has encouraged so many people around the world and has the potential to be a Lifetime movie. I travel the world speaking, motivating others to do the work of healing their inner pain and empowering them to push for a more fulfilling life. I sing and have produced my first CD which is due for release very soon. I am an entrepreneur, teacher and a pastor. My point in all of this, is my life today is worth more than taking it away. In fact, it held the same value as it did back then, I just couldn't see it.

I encourage people to seek out help. Use the resources such as this one, to educate yourself. Set up accountability structures and support systems that are actively apart of your life. The worst thing is needing help and having people who don't know how to journey with you. I am a big advocate of counseling. Seek out a counselor and make this a part of your self-care. See a physician to ensure there are no chemical imbalances that will put a person at a higher risk. Take care of your body; treat it well so it will return the favor to you. Love yourself, counseling will help with this. It's all about being the best care taker of your own life so you can save your life.

Gewanda J. Parker

Author of It Only Hurts When I Can't Run

Pastor, leader, teacher, trainer.

UnSung Heroes

In a perfect world

the homeless would be fed

the injured would be healed

the blind would be led

the depressed would be uplifted

the lost would be found

the scared would be courageous

the illnesses wouldn't be contagious

the rich would share

the poor would learn

there'd be such a thing as fair

the criminals would stop

we would respect all the cops

But we don't live in a perfect world

we live in reality

& often our vision is blurred

we simply cannot see

beyond the confusion, the buzz & the hype

beyond the material, beyond the sad night

For in a perfect world, we would find a way

to have our voices heard, stand up for what we say

find common ground among the divided lines

try to find peace in these often troubling times

We see it every day, the shootings, the outrage

the images burned into our minds

it's happening all the time

-Jessica D. Comer

Chapter 12

A Creative Crushed/Vibrance Returns

by Anonymous

Somewhere, something incredible is waiting to be known.

- Carl Sagan

Depression is like suffocating under the thickest, heaviest blanket. It dulls the senses and swallows you. Sometimes you never want to leave it.

When I'm depressed, I want to be alone, though I'm screaming for help. Sometimes, I hide under blankets in bed or wrap up in a bathrobe and sit in the back of the closet just to feel like I'm safe. I never told anyone except my current husband that I wanted to die.

I've always been creative, a writer, good at nearly everything I did. I fell into depression off and on through college, and it deepened when I couldn't carve out my place in the world as I had hoped, even after my hard work obtaining three degrees. I had failed. Because I had nothing to live for, I frequently thought about ending my life.

I knew I was smart, but I couldn't find a way out of my job. Writing jobs were so rare that I stuck with the ones I had for ten years, despite being treated poorly by my coworkers. In my spare time, I wrote book after book, but no one wanted to publish them, and people rolled their eyes when I told them about my dream. I plotted about starting a business so I could escape the office, but I believed that no one would ever pay me to be creative.

I also had a lot of health problems. I grew up with bad allergies that worsened over the years. I also broke my back when I was 27. I didn't see a doctor when I fell because I thought it was just a bad bruise. I could get over it. It was just me. I wasn't that important.

My first marriage ended a few months after I broke my back, leaving me completely alone. Seeking culture, I moved to Pittsburgh in 2008. I quickly found friends in the salsa community, but I fell into worse depression once I realized that my new job that combined my love for science and writing was crushing me further. The work allowed little creative freedom, and many of the federal employees were brutal. They blamed the contractors for anything that went wrong and would speak to us rudely if they wanted to. I was told to watch every word I said so I didn't make someone angry. It was maddening.

Being alone at home and not connecting with my fellow employees worsened my depression. Despite the friends I made salsa dancing, I thought I was doomed to live alone. Who would want someone so physically broken and with no direction?

I spent long evenings sobbing on the floor in my townhouse dreading sleep because it brought worktime closer. Then I would lie on the floor crying in the morning. I was constantly exhausted, wanting any escape from my life. I always felt like I was wrapped in a thick blanket of lead cotton.

My friends didn't seem to understand my depression. I also saw a therapist for a couple years who helped me tremendously, but I never fully healed.

Stress from work worsened my health. I experienced frequent ocular migraines (a migraine with a light show that blinds you for 30 minutes) and was prescribed emergency migraine meds. When I tried a new one, I felt strange. I debated whether I should call 911 immediately or wait to see if I was really having an allergic reaction to the medicine. Who would care if I died anyway?

I started dating the man I eventually married in late 2009. Within a couple months, my depression improved. He was supportive and listened to me, whether I was up or down. He still does, and I'm thankful for that.

By early 2010, I also began having problems with my digestive system thanks to poor treatment at work and a move to a new noisy office. My employer refused to provide a quiet workspace to write. When I wasn't at work, I obsessed about escape.

In late 2010, I was diagnosed with irritable bowel syndrome (IBS) and saw doctors to determine why I felt like I was being strangled at work. I arrived feeling ok, and by 10 am, the tightness began. Nerves were to blame.

My prescription to dull the nerves in my digestive system—which helped with the strangling sensation and the IBS—had side-effects. I was typically quiet, but on this medicine, I spoke to anyone with the ease of a politician. It was like having a second personality. The medicine also made me stutter when I got nervous and caused one of my eyelids to droop.

In the middle of 2011, I was told to start working from home and soon stopped my stomach meds. Today, though, my emotions are still dulled, and I stutter sometimes when I'm stressed.

Although my back pain, ocular migraines, and digestive issues improved at home, I had new stressors. I knew the federal employees didn't like contractors working offsite, so I carried a huge workload to prove I was doing my part. In my strange trapped freedom, I couldn't leave my desk: someone might email or call to check up on me. Fear of being fired kept me depressed.

Giving birth to two beautiful daughters surprisingly worsened my depression again. I'm usually home with the girls while my husband works evenings. I didn't know anyone nearby with small children, and all my friends seemed busy. Especially after my first was born in November of 2012, I was so lonely that sometimes I would just hold her and cry. She wasn't a very loving baby, and she cried through most evenings. I felt like a servant at work and at home. My life was very dark.

Hip pain prevented adequate sleep during the second half of each pregnancy. The limp that I had worked for years to get rid of returned with both pregnancies but was much worse with the second. My second daughter was induced at 39 weeks because I could barely walk.

Thankfully, she was more cheerful and loving, which prompted my oldest to become cuddlier. But as the end of my second maternity leave approached, I felt sick with fear and apprehension of returning to work. I didn't know how I was going to last until retirement without another substantial break from that agony.

With continued stress at work came a long recovery from pregnancy. Although I lost weight quickly, I hated what I saw in the mirror. It didn't help that my hips were so sensitive that wearing jeans brought on excruciating pain for nearly a year postpartum.

In late 2015, a new director at work led to budget cuts in public affairs. Half the contractor staff was laid off with only two weeks' notice. They called me in on my baby's first birthday, January 6th, and lied about why I was selected. No other writers worked from home. I knew.

For a long time afterward, I was severely depressed. If I worked onsite anywhere, my health problems would return. Because my husband, a sitter, and I switch off on childcare, I couldn't just accept a job somewhere and go without enrolling the girls in daycare.

Thankfully, friends encouraged me to start my own business, and four months later, I finally believed in myself. So many people have said, "I need to talk to you about my book," asked for advice, thanked me for helping them, and recommended me to others. I wish I had done this sooner.

I know my future will make me happy. I finally feel like I am in control, like I'm worth something. I can build an empire.

When I started my business earlier this year, editing books (which I love) helped me become determined to succeed. Until I finished college, I lived to learn. I had goals. After college, there was nothing new to learn. I could only be a technical writer. I was judged but never encouraged. Now, with my own business, I learn new things and thrive on challenges. I have no limits.

If you're thinking about ending your life, remember that someone loves you, even if you don't realize it. Live for them if you can't live for yourself. Your life may be dark right now, but if you stop here, how will you know the end of the story? You can write that ending. Discover your passion, and focus on it. Find something you want to achieve.

Talk to a therapist, life coach, business coach, or someone else who can help you improve your situation. Don't stay trapped within the negative self-chatter or judgement of others. Take action.

Everyone falters at some point. Some go beyond simply stumbling and fall into deep depression. They are not weak. They need a little guidance, a kind word, a helping hand. Show them compassion. You can change their path.

Chapter 13

From the Pits; I Rise

by Melanie Smith-Taylor

The thief comes to steal, kill, and destroy.

- John 10:10a

I always heard, felt, and believed that I wasn't good enough, pretty enough or that I didn't fit in anywhere with anyone. To a lesser degree that's still true; adding to my press to believe God and trust in him in every area of life.

One of the questions asked in my phone interview with Kristie was, "When did you first recognize in your teenage years the change in your mood?" It was before then. By the time I was seven years old life had been so horrific that I remember lying out in the field, looking into the heavens and watching the clouds go by. I told God, "I will do anything to get out of this, to get out of here and be where you are. It's *got* to be better than here."

By my teenage years my outlook was bleak; my mood dismal. I was here in Maryland against my will, an end result of my mother kidnapping me a week before Christmas in 1974. I didn't want to be with my mother. I felt trapped and hopeless because support was very different in the 60's and 70's than it is today. I remember telling my mother when I was 12 years old and had had enough of her abuse that I was going to call the police on her. What did I do *that* for? Most people turned a blind eye and a deaf ear to the less savory components of life back then anyway. Maybe my teachers did the best they could by giving me after school tasks like grading papers and preparing labs which, of course, reinforced my image as the teacher's pet. My counselor was a life-saver and she encouraged my academic, artistic and athletic prowess but my mother only supported the academic arena though my heart was in art and music, subjects I was forbidden to take after beginning high school. I am only learning these past couple of years to be who God created me to be. Is it any wonder that, selfish as it is, I embraced the idea of dying more than the reality of living?

Over the past few years I reconnected briefly with some people from that earlier life and it was interesting to learn we were all in the same boat, trying our utmost to survive. It's incredible how many of us were suicidal then, but nobody really talked about it either. It was just how life was and we were doing our best to get grown.

In both North Carolina and Maryland I did what the counselors advised and got involved in as much school work and extra-curricular activities as I could, but that didn't solve the issues with home life.

What mother does the kind of stuff to her kid that my mother did to me? Actually just this morning I saw a video where a mom packed her young son's suitcase and put him out for voting for Trump in a school election. That child's heartbreak was soul wrenching to me as I saw him, heard his mother, and had flashbacks of my own roadside traumas with my little red suitcase and black patent leather shoes, standing on the roadside after having pleaded with my mother not to throw me away.

When those assigned by God to care for us do things like this, it's very hard to want to keep living. I cannot pinpoint exactly when death became more palatable than life but thoughts of suicide and self-harm were an undercurrent that colored my life, reflected in my art, stories, and music which were quite dark.

I was deeply into horror novels and movies yet because of my style of dress, level of school involvement and academic/athletic achievement I didn't look like your typical person who was dealing with this depth of pain and level of grief. For those with eyes to see and ears to hear my pain came out in the fierceness of how I engaged in my sports. I can recall hurling my tenpin bowling ball so hard the pins would sometimes shatter or pop off the deck and up the lane. The primal yell that would erupt from my gut when putting my shot or tossing the discus was not about trying to gain more distance but about getting away from my life. I was tired of being told what subjects to study, what to eat and how much, catching a beating when I didn't finish, who to date, and so on.

In music, art, writing, and sports, depression and the specter of death was an on-going theme and by the time of my junior and senior years of high school, into college, the Hemlock Society was coming onto the scene and I got involved in that. My research projects throughout college and graduate school, when I could, centered on suicide, suicidal ideation, the best and cleanest ways to die that's going to hurt somebody because hey, you hurt me, you know? You made life a living hell so I hope my death makes the rest of yours hell too. Somehow suicide has always been a thread running in my family, one of many generational curses.

How someone attempts suicide is not as important to me as the fact that, to them, life hurts so badly that suicide is on the table of options to make life better.

Kristie asked me what did I wish people knew or tried to understand about depression? It's this: be involved in the lives of people you say you love. Love is a verb, an action. Also help people to be who God created them to be. The pressure we put on children and young people to be anything other than what God created them to be in his kingdom story is wrong. It's up to parents to understand that you do not own the little people in your lives. They are on loan to you and your job is to be a good steward and shepherd them in the ways of God, not mold them to be your 'mini-me.' Doing so can do great harm and lead to a sad, depressing place for many reasons as we may look like our folks but we are not supposed to be them or necessarily live their dreams.

When one is feeling low or depressed, this is not a time to medicate, manipulate and control. Be involved in the lives of those God has placed across your path, not to the point of smothering, dictating and controlling a person to make them be what you want them to be, but to support, love, and guide, not dropping the ball, not putting your life, career, friends, etc. ahead of being there for your children.

As a former high school educator, parents, please support your children all the way through. There is no magic age when they no longer need you. Also, adults, keep your promises to all, letting your yes be yes and your no be no. When plans change, step up and say so. Honor your word.

A supportive network is so important to help ward off those I can't get through life feelings and all that entails. Not having strong familial encouragement seemed to play a huge part in the depression that I and my friends felt, as well as my students over the years. Most importantly though, in recovery from depression for me, has been having a real relationship with God, with him finding me and me choosing to follow him and be his disciple. No that didn't instantly solve everything in my life. In fact, it brought a whole new set of challenges but I would not trade where I am in my life now for anything the world has to offer. My relationship with God through Jesus Christ is everything to me.

Finally, for those who believe just as I once did, that suicide is their only option, that's a very self-centered choice. It comes however, from a dark, a desperate place that screams "I've tried everything I know and have dealt with this as long as I can. Since no one is listening and helping, I'm outta here!"

For those left behind or know of someone in trouble, do some introspection. What did/can you do to impact their life? How did/can you stand alongside of them and help? What role did/can you play to let them know they matter to you and, inadvertently, to God?

Don't be shy. Let God use you to influence someone else. Your touch may be just the one needed to change a life.

Chapter 14

Just Believe

by Jennifer Newman

Mental illness is such a hard topic to talk about. You may be battling this disease yourself or trying to support someone else. I commend you, because neither situation is easy. I can say that because I have been on both sides. I have lost people close to me and I have been at the point where I almost lost the battle myself. Let me tell you a little bit about me. I am a wife of a police officer and work for a Fortune 500 company. My proudest accomplishments consist of raising two amazing boys, being a proud military mom and a proud survivor of mental illness.

Yes, I used the words proud and mental illness in the same sentence. This wasn't always the case though. I have just started sharing my story, but have battled depression and anxiety for twenty years. I wasn't ready to share the deep dark secret I tried hiding; I didn't want to admit I needed help. Because of that, I suffered in silence for many years. Every day was full of gloom, fear and loneliness. Basically I had lost control of my life and no longer knew who I really was. There were signs of depression for many years that I just ignored; I figured that's how everyone felt. And then I had my first son, what an amazing, beautiful, perfect child. I was supposed to be excited, bragging, and full of joy and life. Instead I sat at home and cried, and then cried some more. What was wrong with me? I knew I had a complicated delivery, I knew about post-partum depression, but I also knew I was supposed to be happy. As the weeks progressed, the darkness kept getting worse.

What I hadn't shared with anyone was that depression is an illness that runs in my family. Unfortunately, I have an uncle and close friend that just couldn't overcome it. I have seen the lasting impacts that it had on those around them.

To be honest, that has probably been what has saved me. I never want to put my children, family and friends through that ongoing pain. I had a friend that had been through depression herself and encouraged me to see the doctor. I was prescribed anti-depressants and given a name of a counselor. I don't know if I didn't mesh with the counselor or if I just wasn't ready to admit that I needed help, so I just relied on the medication.

Through the years I played what I call the medicine game. I went back and forth to the doctor, trying different medicines until I found the right one for me. (It's very important to understand that the first medicine you try may not work. Science is wonderful, there are so many medications; don't give up after just one.) The medicine helped ease some of that dark lonely feeling, but it was never totally gone. So I decided to try counseling again, and this time I found someone I immediately felt comfortable with.

She helped teach me coping mechanisms. Positive self-talk and inspirational quotes were what helped me most. I constantly use the word 'believe.' I have jewelry as well as pictures around my house. These are a constant reminder for me to *believe* in myself, *believe* I could get better, and *believe* life was worth living for. I finally started to take charge of my life again, or so I thought.

I found that depression doesn't magically go away. It came back, and it came back hard. I was sitting at my son's baseball game one day, and for no reason just started crying. No matter what I did, I just couldn't stop. It was at that moment I decided I had one of two choices. Either I finish the pain myself, or do everything I could to defeat this monster inside of me. Although I felt suicide was the easier answer, I knew that wasn't an option. So back to counseling, back to the doctor, back to wherever I needed to go to begin a full fledge war on this disease. Counseling became more frequent and I finally started digesting the root of my problems and understanding some of the reasons I felt like I did. I used my coping tools and away I went...off to better places.

My son, who was about to be a senior in high school decided to enlist in the Air Force. As a mother you feel that pride, but you also know the reality of how our world could be and the dangers that lie ahead. It was honestly the most frightening thing I could imagine, and right away it allowed the doors to re-open for that monster.

What do I do now? I thought. It started taking a tool on me mentally and then physically. I wouldn't go out, I was having chronic migraines, and I was losing control. But I remembered that dark place I was once in and I never wanted to be there again. I learned that having mental illness wasn't my choice, but how I handled it was. I knew I couldn't do this alone. It was hard, but I reached out to my family and friends. I became part of Air Force support groups. I decided that I wasn't going to worry about being embarrassed or ashamed, and to my surprise no one ever made me feel that way. Everyone was full of love and support and helped me accept the situation. I found a way to love myself again, both the good and bad. Although I know it may be an illness I battle for the rest of my life, I am no longer afraid. I know it's a part of who I am, and in the end has made me a stronger person then I ever thought I could be.

As a society we need to educate people on this topic. People need to feel that this is a subject that they can talk about, a subject that doesn't make anyone ashamed to ask for help. If you know someone that may be suffering from depression, talk to them, ask questions, try to understand that deep dark sadness. But most importantly let them know that you love and support them. Although I may not have showed it, I would not be where I am today without the few close friends and family that were there to support me. Sometimes I needed the space to work things out in my mind. They respected that, but would always reach out to let me know they were there for me. I can never give enough thanks to those 3 friends and family that never gave up on me even when I gave up on myself.

Unfortunately, not everyone has the same happy ending. If you have ever lost someone from this illness it's ok to be angry, I would think that would have to be part of the grieving process. But know they didn't choose to take their own life. One doesn't choose to have depression, just like no one would choose to have cancer, heart disease etc. It's a feeling of anxiety, worthlessness and the deepest darkest sadness you could ever imagine. Please know that this was a disease they just couldn't battle anymore.

If you have found yourself to be in that deep dark place, don't give up. You have choices, you have friends. You just need to make it through one day at a time. Know that today may be bad, but tomorrow will be better. Although you may not feel it, know that you *are* loved and you *are* important. Understand that this is an illness that is part of you and it doesn't make you a bad person. Once you embrace that, you will find joy and love in almost everything you do.

Remember there are people that care about you. Walt Disney has a quote that I try and live by: "Believe in you. That's how you make your dreams come true." Even though I don't know you, your life is important to me and I care. Just believe! I believe in you! Now you just need to believe in you!

Chapter 15

The Depths of Loneliness

by Anonymous

I grew up in Ohio, went to college in West Virginia and moved in Pittsburgh 15 years ago. My hobbies are traveling, attending concerts, cultural events, and trying new restaurants.

I have known many people that committed suicide. It keeps happening, especially in schools. Unfortunately, many adults fail the kids because they do not want to get involved and make it worse. The kids feel like no one cares after already feeling bad about themselves. I don't want people to keep feeling like they have no alternative. I'd like these kids to know most people feel this way at some point, and it gets better.

Kids can be really cruel. Fortunately, as we grow, people mature and aren't as cruel. I went to college and made a lot of great lifelong friends, which I never thought would happen in grade and high school. They can get through it too. We need to remove the stigma associated with mental health issues.

Growing up, I was always pessimistic and depressed. At school the kids weren't nice and it was tough. If you weren't who they thought you should be, they would treat you like garbage. Another problem was I was an only child and around adults most of the time. That meant I was more mature and didn't relate to the other kids. My mom was a teacher who was tired from teaching school all day. By the time she got home, she didn't want to deal with me since she dealt with kids all day. My grandmother died when I was seven, I was extremely lonely once she was gone. My mom did the best she could with all the responsibility she had. My dad was a salesman who was on the road weekly from Monday to Friday. She was short tempered, really strict and I didn't feel lots of love. My mom was also a perfectionist who wanted me to do my best. If I got a B, it often wasn't good enough, which eroded my self-esteem.

High school was very tough. I had fun with my boyfriend and his friends. Unfortunately, I thought everyone else hated me, which made it tough to go to school every day. My mom continued to pressure me about school since I'd be applying to college. I studied way too much and nothing was ever good enough, which again, wore away at my self-esteem. When I was a sophomore my best male friend killed himself, which made me feel even worse.

We had a bereavement counselor at school. My mom also allowed me to see a therapist, which really helped. I have been in and out of therapy now for 20 years and it made all the difference. I talked through difficult things I didn't feel I could talk to anyone else about.

I thought about it almost daily. I thought it would be easier if I did not have to hurt all the time and feel terrible about myself. I did not think anyone would care if I did.

It was great going away to college since no one knew me. I could be whoever I wanted to be and not who others thought I was. I made close friends rather quickly. Karen, Summer and I hung out constantly. It was exciting feeling like I had good friends who liked me for me. Unfortunately, I found out the guy I was dating was seeing Karen behind my back. I spiraled and thought *That's it, I'll never have true friends*.

It was tough when Dave did that, but worse to be stabbed in the back by a friend. At that point, I thought why live because I don't have anything to live for. I turned on depressing music in my room, took a bunch of pills and lay down. After choking on the pills, I had a panic attack and called Summer for help. She came and took me to the hospital.

I felt it was the ultimate betrayal and was sick of people letting me down. I thought it would be easier for everybody if I just wasn't here anymore.

It is an ongoing struggle. You can feel better for a while and then something may trigger a relapse, which may take time to recover from. Patience is key. When someone is having a tough time, you need to support them so they feel someone has their back.

A year after my suicide attempt I saw a therapist and tackled multiple difficult topics. After that, I continued because I did not like being a pessimist and worked hard to become an optimist. As you get older, you realize you don't like everybody, not everybody likes you and that's ok.

In 2011 I worked with my new therapist weekly for 2-3 months. Once I felt better, I went every two weeks and then once a month. I worked really hard on myself that year and finally conquered my demons. It was the best thing I've ever done. Once I found peace within myself, I found my husband, had better relationships with friends and family and become the person I always wanted to be.

I would want them to know that I am a survivor and they can be too. Even when it looks bleak, there is always hope and always someone who cares they could call. If they don't feel comfortable talking to a friend or a family member, they could call a suicide hotline or talk to someone at a church. There is always someone who will listen and help them find new coping strategies to get through it.

Patience, understanding and compassion are the most important things in dealing with someone who has a mental health issue. Know we don't want to feel this way. It is just who we are and we can't help it. We're doing the best we can. Have patience with us. It's tough having anxiety because you stress over things easily. No one wants to worry all the time. We can't help it and are trying the best we can. Some days are not going to be good days, realize that and support us anyway. Telling people to get over it and that it's unproductive to worry so much can be really frustrating and hurtful for the person going through it. What is helpful is someone who truly listens and tells them they are there for them. We understand it is tough to truly empathize if you don't have the same problems, but at least try to sympathize and support us. No one wants to feel this way.

I am proof that by talking things out with someone and constantly working on yourself, you can turn things around. Even if it seems like no one cares and there is no other way, there is always someone who cares and there *is* another way.

During my terrible childhood, I felt like I'd never survive, would never make friends, would never repair things with my family and would never find someone to love, but I did. If someone doesn't feel comfortable enough to talk to the people in their life, there is always someone outside their circle they can confide in. There is always somebody that can help you brainstorm ways to get around whatever bad situation you are dealing with.

Not feeling good enough has been a constant theme my entire life. The Mantra I have been using lately is: "I have everything inside me that I need to be successful."

Chapter 16

Against all the Odds

By Maricel

I am Hispanic/Latino. I was born in Cuba and raised in the Bronx, NY. I had three sisters. We all immigrated here to the United States where I started school and learned English.

I was living a double life for a long time. At home everything was Cuban and Latino culture, but when I stepped out the door it was a different world. It was American. I wore a different dress, used a different language and ate different food. For a long time I just didn't fit in anywhere. In school there were a lot of African Americans and Puerto Ricans, but there weren't that many Afro-

Cubans- people that looked like me or talked like me. Early on I had issues with my identity.

I've never shared my suicide experience. I believe that it may be able to help someone get through it and survive it. I can face those demons now. I can face them today; I have accepted who I am at this point in my life.

I noticed a change in my moods when I was molested. I was molested by a sibling's husband when I was 12 years old. The molestation continued for a long time. When it was exposed, I was blamed and it made me want to run and disappear.

My sister blamed me. She blamed me for ruining her marriage. From that point on I began to run from myself. I didn't like myself. I believed what my sister said was truth. Since I was still a minor and living with my parents, when my sister and her husband would come to the house, I was sent to my room. This affirmed my shame, guilt, and feelings of not belonging. I already had identity issues at school. This confirmed I was the black sheep in the family. I did not want to live because I caused so much pain to the family. I felt so much rejection and self-loathing, that I ran away at age 15 to Times Square. I ran back to my molester's arms and he took me in. While living with him, I attempted to cut myself.

I did not reach out for support because I was a minor runaway. I didn't want to go back to Ohio to my parents' home. I was trapped.

I thought of suicide and harming myself quite a bit. I self-harmed a couple of times. My molester found me cutting and bleeding. I still have a tiny little scar. I attempted suicide twice.

Since my molester was a paraplegic, (and a drug dealer) he had all kinds of medicine. Once, I took all of his medicine and had to have my stomach pumped. Another time I cut myself but I stopped so I didn't go to the hospital. He had a lot to lose by taking me because I was a minor runaway.

I was lonely. I would think about the good times with my mom, dad, and sisters. Then there was the detachment. I couldn't go to school. I didn't fit in. I couldn't tell anyone the life I was living.

There weren't many resources for runaways. I felt powerless. I couldn't fix it. *Why am I here if I don't fit in? I can't go back. I hate where I'm at. I can't go anywhere.* It was like the stage was set for me to be non-existent. I wanted to die. I would use drugs to get me through the feelings but I hated it. I knew a couple of runaways who were strippers. Back then they were called go go dancers. A couple of them died. I wished it would have been me.

I want people to know that they are not alone in their depression. I love technology because it opens up so many doors of community and hope. Depression will make you feel like you're alone in this; like you're not normal. In my upbringing and in my Latin home, it was like something was wrong with me. I was supposed to get over it; just move on. I want people to know they are not alone. It's not an uncommon thing. There are other people that suffer with this stuff too and are living through it. They're surviving it.

I'm a survivor of domestic violence. In between the beatings and trying to raise my children while living with my abuser, I had to get on medication. I thank God that I did. My anxiety was bad. I am not ashamed because it helps. It's ok to talk about it and to take antidepressants. Some people have to live with that for the rest of their lives.

Medication helped, and so did my spirituality. I overcame my depression *through* my spirituality.

My journey to triumph happened when all the pretenses, all the fakeness, all the falseness, pride and ego got knocked off my shoulders. I was looking at the face of a judge and he told me, "There's no place here for your kind unless you get off methadone and you stop shooting up." This was a black judge by the way so it wasn't a racial thing. Never mind that I qualified because I was a first time offender. For me that was a real rude awakening. The first thing that came to my mind was *what's going to happen to my children? I can't go to prison.* I had to come back to report to that judge to see if I did everything he told me to do. I attempted everything on that damn list and I failed, but I showed up at that courtroom. I said I couldn't do it so I left the treatment center and had to go get well because I was dope sick. As a result, I was back on methadone. He looked at me and I was so scared. But he said because I told the truth, he would accept me into this program. See, once I let go of all my false pretenses and just told the truth, that's when it started to happen for me. From that point on, I started to talk about my life. I started going to meetings. I got involved in the 12 steps. I got a sponsor. I journaled. I started to strip myself of all these walls. There is power in numbers and that's when I allowed myself to become vulnerable enough to tell the truth about myself. There was no more pretending. There was no more I couldn't handle. It was like my God put me in a place to be stripped of everything so I could live again.

When a person feels like suicide is their only choice, it is. When I felt it was my only choice, it was! It *really* was. It was the grace of God that he found me in time and I didn't bleed to death. I don't know how he found me with the pills but when I came to, they were pumping my stomach.

If I could speak directly to someone who is in the place that I was in, I would just want to hold them. I don't have a word because what I would want is for someone to hold me. I wouldn't want to hear anyone say anything to me. And if I was crying, I'd want someone to cry with me.

Hold me, cover me and if I'm crying, you cry because that little girl, that 15-year-old runaway, that 16 year old runaway, that 22 year old mother of three little babies, that's what she needed. That's all she ever needed.

I thank God for those who haven't struggled with depression and suicidal thoughts because they are in a good position to be a light to someone who does. I'm already feeling awkward in my own skin. I'm already feeling and questioning my sanity and my abilities but I come to this person (my neighbor) that doesn't have that issue but is willing to teach me and to show me and not laugh at me but support me. It could be the simplest things that are really big to someone struggling because we want to live a normal life. For example, I didn't know how to bake a cake for my children and I didn't have the money to buy them one. You may be surprised to think something so simple brings about depression and anxiety to people like me, but comparing myself to others left me devastated. Well this mom taught me how to bake a cake. It made all the difference for me

I can't emphasize enough that we are made of mind and body. We have a soul. And I can't emphasize enough to people that medication is good, especially if you've gone through what you needed to do to get to that medication that's working for you. Counseling and talking things through is so good. That's where the beginning of my transformation came through and so thank God I was open to that. I was so hungry and so thirsty, so lost, and in so much pain; I hope people don't have go through that to get to that place. So I can't emphasize enough for people to take care of their spirit and their soul.

One of the things I like to remind myself of is God is love. Love does exist and I am loved.

Chapter 17

Now, Why?

by John Allen

Hi my name is John, I drive a London black taxi, I am a man's man. I am strong, hardworking, a great farther, and loving husband.

So *why the fuck* was I standing in the pouring rain, crying, feeling sick on the edge of a cliff? I looked down the water was bashing against the rocks. I was going to jump thinking *I must take a run at it. The pain will be over soon; the 'why' will stop.* I looked again but I didn't feel the cold. I didn't feel anything really, my mind, my inner-voice screamed *Why? Why does this always happen to me, Why are the voices in my head so loud, why am I losing everything, why is life so shit?*

Now I could tell you all about how my childhood was a total fucking mess. I could tell you how I was raped when I was 8 years old at knife point. I could tell you how the house I lived in was a war zone every day. How I left school with no qualifications, how at, 13 my father told me he did not want me around anymore.

My teenage years consisted of drugs and other addictions. But truthfully, none of that mattered at that point. It was not directly happening while I stood there planning to take my own life.

It was just me and my inner-voice standing in the pouring rain on the edge of the cliff.

That inner-voice was getting louder and louder. *You're no fucking good. You have fucked your whole life up. You're going to lose everything* . The loudest and the most hurtful on was *Your world has fallen apart*. I could hear this crystal clear; loud and sharp but there was no one else there, just me.

Something happened next that I did not understand at the time, but makes total sense now. I ran and I jumped. I felt myself falling. I could hear the wind as I fell towards the rocks . It was a very long drop, 100- 200 feet down. It went in slow motion then- *crack*. I felt every bone in my body break, I felt my head cave in; sharp pain through my body. It was over.

I stood at the top of the cliff and looked down at my broken body on the rocks. My legs turned to jelly. I sat on the bench next to me and cried like I had never done before.

I was starting to come around, come to my senses or wake up. I was still a total mess but I felt lighter. The fear of facing my past demands was still in my head. The voice had changed though. The language was different. It was saying *You need to get your head sorted.*

I got back in my taxi which was parked behind me and drove home, crying all the way. I was terrified of having to face the past and deal with it. Dealing with the demands started by talking opening up and being honest. Honest to myself and to the people who mattered to me (my wife Claire).

Claire was the one I hurt the most; she had no idea of what had gone on, how I felt over the years. I had become an expert at hiding my feelings and not talking about my emotions. Well that's what a man should do? That's what I thought. How wrong I was.

I went and got professional help in the form of a psychiatrist. His diagnosis was post-traumatic stress disorder (PTSD). He said I would need 2 years of therapy. My troubles were buried deep down.

He asked me If I read. I didn't but I told him I'd give it a go. So he told me to go off and read *A Road Less Travelled* by M. Scott Peck. I read it and was gripped, this book was speaking a language I could understand. It was like he went into my mind and started giving me answers to the question 'why.'

At my next session I asked for another book and was given *The Power of Now* by Eckhart Tolle. After six sessions and six books I decided reading gave me all the help I needed so I stopped the therapy and the books became my guide.

Six years on from the edge of the cliff I have read over three hundred books on mindfulness, neuroscience, neurobiology, psychology, NLP, and body language.

I have my answers to those 'why' questions and have taught myself how to quieten that inner-voice or make it speak the language that I want to hear.

A very important lesson I learned from my studies is that if I did not survive and had not made it, the pain would not have died with me. All I would have done is passed it to my loved ones, passed it to my wife and children.

In a strange way I *did* jump, I *did* die but I came back stronger and found myself.

My favorite poem is *If* by Rudyard Kipling. It's how I would like to live my life.

Chapter 18

Out of the Shadows of Wealth

by Becca Buffer

I am a 21-year-old female named Becca Buffer. I'm pursuing a career in social work at a community college. My plan is to transfer to the University of Pittsburgh in the beginning of 2017. I grew up north of Pittsburgh; the suburbs. I lived in a financially stable home with caring, but strict parents. I have three brothers and I am the second born. My childhood was very enriching, mostly supportive in a loving environment.

I did suffer from anxiety at a very young age which developed into depression in the long run. As a child, I was diagnosed with a learning disability, which did interfere with my confidence, but as I grew older I realized it does not define who I am as a person. It's so important for me to share my story now because I have become emotionally stronger and a more independent woman than I was before. I embrace being vulnerable. Vulnerability will make a difference to those not able to express their feelings and awareness to suicidal thoughts.

As early as I can remember, I suffered from anxiety. At the time, I thought it was normal for all children to feel the way I felt. When

I got older, I thought it could be my hormones after going through puberty, but my anxious feelings never let up. At the age of 16, I started having relentless visions of causing a fatal car accident while driving. These visions would be so intense I had to stop driving for months. I would talk to my mother about it because she witnessed my suffering while I drove. She realized my anxiety was affecting my mood and made an appointment with a psychiatrist. This drastically helped me with my mood. The only support I received after the age of 16 were close friends and my therapist that I started going to at the age of 18.

My parents were and still are supportive of me, I just kept my feelings from them. I hate for people to worry about me because I am more of a giving person than a receiving person.

During my first week as a sophomore at college, I had police knocking at my dorm door. When I think back to this emotional, dark time, it was the best thing that happened to me. The police came for a self-harming case. I thought to myself, *I have been hiding my depression and anxiety for so long, how could I get caught now?* With a rage of tears, I confessed to the police that I was suicidal. Thankfully my parents came to pick me up in the middle of the night. If they couldn't, I would have been sent to the hospital. This was a time when support came to me, and I will forever be thankful to those kind officers, the acquaintance that brought it to the officer's attention and the support I had from my family and friends.

During this time in my life, suicide was often a daily thought. Some days were better than others, some weeks were better than others. It depended on my mood and environmental factors. My mood was tremendously fragile during this time period. At my lowest of low, I would resort to self-harm. I would break down and surrender to my demons. I felt completely hopeless, depressed, exhausted, and uneasy. My mind was filled with darkness. The feeling is so deep, so dark, and so debilitating. I was entirely detached from reality. I can honestly say I hated myself. I felt worthless to the world. I wasn't good enough for my family and friends. I felt like I was burden to others. Some days I would vigorously cry and others I would have no feeling at all. I would always imagine my funeral, and what it would be like with me gone. I would self-harm when I felt I wouldn't get caught. Since I had anxiety surrounded around others finding out, I would do it mainly a couple times a month.

My mood really depended on how often I self-harmed. I have never truly attempted suicide but I had many nights where I would wish I wouldn't wake up, or I would drink a little too much or I would 'accidently' get hit by a bus or car. I had constant thoughts of ways I could end my life. I felt that ending my life I was saving myself from my intense dark thoughts and anxiety filled moments. It was as though I was doing myself and the world a favor.

For people that haven't experienced depression, it can be difficult to fully comprehend what the person is going through. I want others to know that depression isn't something that can be switched on and off. The depressed person can't just 'toughen up.'

Depression is a mental illness that many people suffer from. For people to understand mental illnesses better, I always relate it to being physically ill. Most of the time when someone is experiencing an infection, they have to receive antibiotics. Physical illnesses can't be treated by ignoring them. This is the same with mental illness. Mental illness is just as serious. It is a real feeling that people experience. It is so important to remember that each person experiences depression in different ways.

The best decision I made to overcome my depression was moving back home from college. Home was a place where I felt safe and had endless support and love. I surrounded myself around positivity. I even let go of friendships that didn't serve me. I gravitated towards people that were more like me. I took steps to better my mental health by visiting my psychiatrist and starting weekly therapy. I began to meditate and attend yoga classes to make a connection between my mind and body. During my recovery, I did a lot of soul searching. I found things that fed my soul and made me genuinely happy. With this, I found who I am as person.

Thinking back to who I was and who I am now brings tears to my eyes. I am proud to say that I am not the person who I used to be. In therapy, we discussed how I evolved into a strong, positive young woman. Although my recovery process was slow, I can finally say I *have* made it! I *have* a purpose, and I *am* worthy of all things beautiful. I can truly say I love myself.

If you have a loved one that struggles with depression or suicidal thoughts try to understand their position. Show love and care to those who are suffering. It is hard to understand, but provide the support they need and guide them to reach out for help. Take your loved one's condition seriously.

Imagine this: you are holding a cup of water out in front of your body. Hold this cup of water for a couple minutes. Easy right? Now hold this cup of water for weeks at a time. Imagine how draining this could be. This is depression.

To those of you that feel ending your life is your only choice I want you to know that you're loved. Don't give up, you are needed on this earth. You too have a purpose. Don't be afraid to reach out for help. I don't personally know what you are going through but I promise you will blossom out of the darkness.

My favorite quote is "With brave wings, she flies." I have a tattoo with this quote and a beautiful feather on my hip. This quote is a reminder of how strong I am and to continue fighting.

I have a huge thanks to my mama and my boyfriend. My mama gave me great motherly support and love. She is the star that lights up my life. Our relationship means so much to me. Thank you Mama, I love you. My boyfriend has truly helped me rise above the darkness and see the light. He supported and still supports me every step of the way. Thank you D. I love you forever and always.

A special thanks to Kristie Knights for supporting and showing endless care for me. You have truly saved me and have helped me beyond words. You're an inspiration. You are my hero. I am forever thankful for you.

Chapter 19

The Phoenix Rising

by Jessica D. Comer

I am a daughter, sister, aunt, friend, girlfriend and suicide attempt survivor. I am diagnosed with depression, anxiety, PTSD, and bipolar disorder. I went through a phase in my life in which I lived in darkness, searching for the light. Traumatic events were occurring at such a rampant pace that my mind was put on overload and my spirit was practically shut down.

On a beautiful day in May of 2013, I found myself alone in a neighbor's field with a brand new razor. I looked to the sky, I called to God. I spoke softly of the life I was prepared to end. Then I began slicing my wrists and throat.

It was a brutal suicide attempt. Suddenly I heard a tractor, looked around and saw my neighbor coming towards me. He hoisted me onto his tractor, pulled out a cell phone and called 9-1-1. I was crying, bleeding, screaming. I begged him to get a gun and finish me off. I saw my parents in the distance and the reality of what I had just done overwhelmed me. I begged him not to let them see me in such a terrible physical state. As the sirens blared, the emergency workers cut my clothes off and worked diligently tending to my multiple wounds. They were calm as they spoke to me, encouraged me, and shared their stories with me.

During my hospital stay, I had so many visitors. Family and friends showed up constantly to support, love, and be with me. I had a sense of guilt because several other patients never had visitors. No one showed up to be by their side.

I had spent seven years working at a comprehensive victim's service agency. Of those seven years, I spent three and a half counseling people. So during my hospital stay, I chose to get to know other patients. We talked, checked out videos on YouTube, listened to music, wrote letters, stories, and poetry, and so on.

Here I am, three and a half years later, sharing my story of survival. So why share this horrific experience now? I find myself at a crossroads in my life at which I feel compelled to help others who are in darkness. As a survivor, I know that the darkness only lasts so long. Eventually, the sun shines again. Sometimes we have to choose it and find the light, but it's always there. It lives right inside of you.

I believe in living life with kindness, compassion, and empathy. We are all worthy. We all matter. Sometimes we all have to dance in the rain before the rainbow shines.

Personally, I have a few life mantras that I utilize daily:

Inhale the future, exhale the past.

Jeremiah 29:11. For I know the plans that I have for you says the Lord plans to prosper you and not to harm you. Plans to give you hope and a future.

I cannot change the past, I am focused on the future.

Depression can be a crippling ailment. It can certainly be something that blinds you to joy. It makes you feel defeated, depleted, unworthy. I never considered myself to be someone with mental health issues, just a quirky individual with a loud, boisterous attitude. But I hit very hard times that took a toll on my mentality and the sun stopped shining. I was definitely depressed. But I try to keep myself and my life balanced. I volunteer. I write. I try to remain active in various ways, contributing in life when I can. I've even been lucky enough to fall in love with an incredible man who I feel is my soulmate. He challenges me and helps me move forward.

Writing is my passion, the fuel to my fire. I'm finally proud of the poetry that I create. I went through a time when I never felt it was good enough. But it's a great outlet for me and seems to occur quite naturally. I enjoy it immensely and feel incredibly humbled when it is appreciated and people can relate. I write from personal experiences, observation, fantasy, etc.

I am proud and excited to be a part of this book project. If my story or any of my poems help even one person to move out of the shadows & into the light, then it's worth it to me. Suicide is *never* the answer. There is always hope, things will indeed improve, and we are all vital, unique individuals. Stay positive, love and be kind to yourself, and always remember that you are not alone in this life.

Chapter 20

Expected Strength

by Leslie

I'm guessing that everyone loves a blue sky; what's not to love about corn-blue skied, cloudless days with summer sounds of kids laughing, birds chirping, cars whizzing by your open window? Everyone is heading somewhere, people are busy living their lives, happy, smiling faces head off to the park, the zoo, the Carnegie Museum.

But me? I'm curled up in my bed with the curtains closed, my head hurts from too much alcohol the night before and I can't decide if I don't want to get up because I have a hang-over or if I don't want to get up because I just don't want to live anymore.

I'm lonely, I'm sad, I hurt in my heart, in my head in my body, I don't cry because I don't cry but I want to cry and it just won't come out. It won't come out because I'm strong, I'm a go-getter, I'm a do-er, I pay my bills, I love my kid, I go to work every day and smile and laugh and I'm a wonderful, committed employee and boss. People love me but people don't know me. I'm a black cloud living in a blue sky day and I don't know if I can do it anymore.

It's exhausting being three people, or maybe I'm more than that. I'm loving mom, I'm screaming-mad mom, I'm get your god-damn homework done mom, I'm IEP mom who doesn't even know what that means but damn it I will *not* let on that I don't know and I will go home and research it – unless I drink first and then maybe tomorrow.

My mom persona is always trying to find the balance between strict discipline and fun – usually strict mom wins out because Dad, the ex-husband, is a fun person and we can't possibly have two fun parents with a wild child – someone has to teach this kid manners, rules, right from wrong and I guess that has to be me.

So black cloud mom is miserable, cranky, not fun and I think my kid knows it, and I hate that I think she knows it, and I try harder to be fun mom so we go to friend's houses and play, we go camping and hike in the woods at Moraine State Park, Ohiopyle and even Trillium Trail brings a smile to her face, but my face? My face is cracked and forced and as much as I love to see my child happy, I don't really feel happy but I can't let her know that because she might think she is to blame and she isn't. It's me.

My super boss, super employee persona is equally as exhausting as super mom persona. I come to work on time, if not a little early. I try to stay late but I have to get my child from day care so I don't take a break because I need to get things done.

My customers love me, how can they not? I remember what they wore, when they wore it, the occasion they bought it for, I call them for the sale on the skirt they wanted, I hand write thank you notes and make cute comments about things we talked about – they see me in the street and the grocery store and say "Hi!" but my head says I'm faking it, I'm not really happy doing all of this, I'm not really that good at remembering all this detail, how does that happen? Who am I? How did I get into this retail industry? I wanted to work with blind people for God's sakes, I wanted to be a police officer and work with rape victims, I wanted to help people for crying out loud - and here I am selling expensive clothing to really nice, rich people with a few bitches interspersed to make the day go just a little quicker. Boy did we like it when the bitches came in – we had so much to talk about after, but did my staff really know me? Hell no.

If I'm really honest with myself, the wild child persona was the most exhausting and if I'm really thinking about someone to blame – it's her. Goddammit – it's her – the crazy, wild-woman, the drinking, smoking, slutty, sleep around drunk girl who loved to drink before she left home to prime and not pay so much in bar bills, was a hot mess after she dated the waiter who introduced her to Manhattans, and drove home drunk more times than she can remember.

Referring to my wild child in the third person distances me from her. I put her into a box and taped the lid when I met Dan. Thank God I met Dan, really, I thanked God I met Dan a lot in the beginning; now we argue about money and kids just like everyone else. But Dan hasn't seen me curled up in ball on a blue skied Saturday afternoon when we are all supposed to be outside playing. Sure he has seen me curled up in a ball from a hangover, but the black cloud day, the darkness that was in my head that day, the feeling that everything hurt, nothing could be repaired, nothing could change, I'm full of shit and no one even cares to help me work through my insecurities; he hasn't seen that day, thank God.

Genetically, depression runs in my family and so does alcoholism so it really isn't, or shouldn't be, any surprise to me or really to anyone else in my family that I had a depressed period of my life. My grandmother was an alcoholic, my biological dad committed suicide and I will never know who he is, I don't even want to, but as I typed that sentence I realize that maybe I'm faking that too.

That afternoon of not wanting to leave my bed, ever, that period of my life albeit brief, was the one time that I remember thinking *I could die today. I could die today and it would be ok because there are beautiful blue skies outside, my child is with her dad, he is the fun parent and it will be ok. People like the me they think they know, so it will be ok – they'll miss me and remember the good times, they'll laugh and say "Oh she was so much fun – remember when…?"*

Somehow, instead of taking that thought and formulating a plan of action towards suicide, I called a friend. I called my ex-boyfriend, the one guy who was a sweet boy, a loving caring guy who wanted to meet my daughter but I pushed him away because I didn't think my daughter and I were ready. I called Tom and he talked to me with such kindness, he talked to me about the blue sky, he talked to me about opening the curtains and letting in the light, he gently asked me to stand by the window and breathe.

I got mad, I said "I can't do that, I can't move, I don't want to move, it's miserable in my head, everything hurts" and he said "You sound depressed."

It was the first time that anyone had ever said such a thing to me and I know that the strong girl had to kick in, the bad-ass mom, the perfect boss, the greatest employee persona's had to take over. They were the ones who had to drag the sorry-assed, drunk girl out of bed, that had to make her move, the 'get on with it' mentality, the 'pull up your boot-straps' woman was the only way to move forward.

All three of my personas do not get depressed and somehow that word depression kicked me into high gear. Sweet Tom, he gave me a phone number for a doctor that he thought I should talk to, he said "I'm sure you will like her, she is like you, no nonsense." I thought, *Right, that's me, no nonsense. Now get the heck out of this bed and get a glass of water and some Advil. It's going to be ok.*

Chapter 21

Innersprings of a Soul

by Vimala Pooja

My name is Vimala Pooja. I am a social activist by profession who works with working children and women. I felt that sharing my story will help others. I wanted to contribute my story as an inspiration for others to prevent suicide.

I never knew how, or had an opportunity to share my story in the past. This seems like the best platform.

I am a very sensitive person. When I was 13 years old I had mood swings and suicidal thoughts. Poverty and family situations made me like that, by suppressing my thoughts very often and suffering inside. I never reached out or shared with anyone that I had such thoughts. I had racing thoughts, thoughts of hopelessness and helplessness most of the time.

Right now I do not have thoughts of suicide. However, from the age of 13, I have attempted suicide five to six times in my life, all by over dosing. With each attempt I increased the number of pills I took from 10 tablets to 80 tablets in the final attempt.

Reasons were different at each stage of life. I did not know how to cope up with my life. I suffered for years; alone and silent. I was trying and trying to end my life.

Sometimes I used to wonder why it was so difficult to die. I had attempted so many times, only to be saved. The 6th attempt was a life changing event for me. I did not want to be a failure this time; I took 80 gardenal sodium pills. I was in the ICU for 10 days in a critical condition, but I lived. I never told anyone about my overdose.

I couldn't walk properly and was required to attend physiotherapy for two months.

Being a self-made and independent woman living with a psychopath husband is like leading a life walking on a tight rope. It forces one to have severe negative thoughts to the extent of suicide. I suffered from a major depressive disorder. I was under treatment for two years. No matter how hard I tried to get better; I couldn't. Finally, I ended up with suicide, I felt this was the only solution to all my problems.

The doctor who gave me treatment changed my life. His simple caring, pleasant attitude, and positive words brought a huge change in my life. He encouraged me to continue my studies and work for a cause. Following his advice, I did my masters in sociology. I joined a social organization. I worked for the people. I helped thousands and thousands of people who were in such situations for 10 years. It brought me immense satisfaction.

Of course I continued to have psychiatric and medical treatments for my health condition. As I was absent from my work for two months due to my treatment, the organization for which I worked gave me notice stating disciplinary action for being absent.

If one is in the stage of ending his or her life, where is time to think about work? For one year this problem went on and finally that was solved. From then onwards whenever I felt low in life I diverted my mind by studying a new course. It has helped me succeed professionally and personally. It's not that I have fully eradicated the depression and anxiety I have suffered. But, I have learned to cope with life. I have also learned to live life in all situations; that is the difference.

I want to tell people with suicidal thoughts to share whatever feelings you have with your trusted people or help groups. Please get help as early as possible. We all are there for a purpose; not to end life. Treat this problem as any other health problem. Eradicate it from life. Ending life is not the solution to problems. Instead facing life in all circumstances is the true essence of life.

I took many steps to heal myself. Here is what helps me:

- Being yourself and doing the things you like.

- Listening to music helps a lot.

- Being with family and friends.

- Walking in parks, nature and serene environments.

- Being with positive people.

- Awareness and reading stories of people who travelled in this path soothes and helps to heal a lot.

- Talking or being with people who attempted suicide helps as a moral boost and heals our inner-self in immense ways when we are struck in a vicious circle and unable to come out of it.

- Seeking treatment with psychiatrists and counsellors also helps in the healing process.

- Stay occupied.

- Working with similar kind of people helping them to solve also heals us.

Having undergone various trials and tribulations in life in a positive way it gives immense emotional strength to the mind to face life.

I want to tell people who think suicide is the only choice that life is beautiful. Your life doesn't revolve around one person or one situation where you go to such extremes.

If you have gone through some failures in relationships or failure in any other things in life, suicide cannot be an option. New people, new opportunities, new circumstances will always be available to us; we just have to identify it.

See and learn from the weaver bird building its nest. You will learn a lot for your life. Watch how many times the nest falls to the ground, every time he gets up and builds a new nest until he completes it. So whenever you fail or fall in life always rise, rise, and rise to live a life.

Chapter 22

My Soul Found the Light

by Suzanne Sammon

Years ago, my parents took me and my best friend to upstate New York for a visit with my aunt and uncle. They lived on a mountain and engaged in a pioneer-type style of existence. I was very intrigued by their cabin, water pump, and cooking stove.

After a couple of enjoyable hours of conversation, my aunt stated to me and my friend, "Would you like to see our cave?" Both of us looked at each other, trying to figure out if we heard her right. She went on to explain that the cave was their "Refrigerator and freezer." Needless to say, we were very captivated and curious about this cave. My aunt encouraged us to bring a sweater or jacket due to the temperature change. We took a trail behind their cabin and then had to hike down a sloping hill. I felt the cold immediately as we walked closer to our destination.

Nothing could have prepared me, though, for the huge, gaping, black hole that suddenly appeared in our vision. It was overwhelming! My adventurous friend wanted to go inside and explore, but that was not allowed due to safety issues. My aunt went on to explain how they rigged a contraption to store their food and then hoist it up to the trail above. It was mind-boggling to say the least.

As I reflected on this experience, I was amazed at how this cave paralleled some of my particular life journeys. Some periods were like the steady trail that was above the cave with comfortable temperatures and safe elements. Other periods echoed the frigidity and downward direction towards the cave. Suicidal thoughts and attempts reflected the suffocating darkness all around me.

When the brain is traumatized and overpowered by circumstances, disappointments, rejections, and broken dreams, it becomes like that cave- total blackness and not being able to see anything supportive, familiar, or helpful. It is when we receive glimpses of light that we can start to see beyond what is holding us in fear and stagnant thinking. This is what happened to me.

My mother told me recently that I was born brave. She said this in response to a statement I made where I felt like so much of my life has been a fight for survival, and how exhausted I was feeling. She referenced this to the time I was hospitalized at three years old for severe asthmatic complications (this was the beginning of several hospitalizations due to asthma). The pediatrician pulled no bones about the fact that I had a fifty/fifty chance of living. I do not have children, but I can only imagine what that statement did to my parents' minds and hearts.

Back then, I was put in an oxygen tent and had very limited human contact. My mother was there by my side, but to be wrapped in plastic for days was horrifying. (I believe this is part of my claustrophobia.) I could not even watch TV because the sparks from the electricity could have ignited a fire or explosion with the tent. I endured several blood gas treatments, and that pain went beyond anything I ever experienced, as it goes right into your artery. Yet, I never complained, according to my mother. She said I was a true warrior.

I must confess that I have often questioned God on why he kept me alive that week? It was not the first time that I was near death, as I was involved in a dreadful car accident due to a teen running a red light.

As a young child, I was subjected to many abusive actions by peers and adults. One of the most appalling episodes that took place in school, of all places, was when I was working on an art project, and we had to write the words New Jersey on the paper. This particular teacher stopped at my desk and noticed an error in how I spelled Jersey. Instead of whispering to me about my mistake, she grabbed the paper off of my desk, shouted to the class, "Look who misspelled New Jersey," and tore it to shreds.

I developed early as a female, and by middle school, the boys were calling me disgusting names and pulling my bra strap or trying to touch me. I played a musical instrument in my last years of elementary school, but by the time I got to seventh grade, the band teacher informed my parents that I was not good enough for the performing band. By the time I reached high school, I aspired to be in theatre, but was told my singing voice was not at the level to be selected. Tenth grade was when I first attempted suicide. I had had enough.

There were many more thoughts throughout my early adulthood. I also began my 'coping' technique of self-mutilation. At the time, I was working a retail job and had my own box cutter. After an upsetting moment at work one day, I went into the bathroom, took out the blade, and cut myself. For years, I thought I was the only one doing this, and it wasn't until I was a social worker that I realized a lot of other people had been struggling with the same behavior. Wonderful souls who, like myself, were so wounded by situations, but these were wounds we could control.

It was during the decade of my thirties that I had an attempt which landed me in the hospital. It may seem terrifying, but it was the beginning of my healing journey. It was the first light in my emotional cave. I met so many individuals who could relate to what I was feeling and dealing with. I learned about depression and trauma. I spoke with staff who understood and gave hope that life was, indeed, worth living. I wasn't crazy; my brain was overloaded, and it just became too much to handle. I am not ashamed that this is part of my story.

Outpatient therapy was part of the treatment plan, and while there were a few in between, I was blessed with an amazing, compassionate therapist for seven years before she had to take a full-time position. My sessions with her allowed me to open up about situations that had been deeply buried for years. She was there for me during some heart-wrenching life events, including losing my dad to a heart attack, cancer scares, a fibromyalgia diagnosis, nerve damage complications from the prior car accident, a divorce, and family addictions, including hoarding. She also worked with me in stopping the self-mutilation. Whenever she had to offer another point of view, she did it with absolutely no judgment. She was an angel in every sense of the word.

Amidst the struggles and challenges, many blessings have come about. I was able to obtain three college degrees, including a master's degree. I have traveled extensively and participated in many volunteer activities. I served in the American Red Cross and was chosen to speak at a global conference regarding disasters and mental health. I have been selected for leadership positions and been in management at previous jobs. I have been a public speaker on many occasions, and my photography is getting well-known on social media. Do I still have rough days? Yes, I do. Do I still question God? Yes, but not the same question as before. I realized through prayer, personal development and my support system that there was a purpose in God keeping me alive when I was three and then after the accident. My pain is being transformed into something even bigger than I could ever think of or imagine. While I would never want to repeat a lot of what I endured, I am allowing it to help others from making a permanent, fatal choice. Life *is* worth living, and celebrating victories along the way, even small ones, can lift one up even on the worst of days.

The cave can be scary-looking, but there is always a light. Sometimes we have to adjust our focus or change our location, but it is possible to get through. There is no darkness that can overtake the light. Love and hope will prevail if we just allow it to happen.

Chapter 23

Endless pain, Now Sustained

by Sheri Allen

I grew up in a small town in Western New York. I grew up in a home where my parents got along but I was the child that was either invisible or else I couldn't do anything right. My brother was always the perfect child, and because of this my mom and I fought on a regular basis. It was also a home where asking for help was admitting you were weak. You didn't ask for help in my family. You just needed to suck it up and deal with it. In my family, you didn't share your secrets with each other. Little did I know how much that would hinder my journey in this life.

It is important to share my story now so that others can learn from what I went through and find hope. There is hope and the suicidal thoughts will pass. There are also ways to deal with what you are going through. Each person has a purpose in this life. I survived and you can too.

I first recognized the changes in my mood when I was younger. It all came to the surface with the passing of my mom. With her passing I sank into a deep pit of depression and things began to spiral out of control. I couldn't deal with the loss of my mom and

I blamed myself for the horrible words I had with her. The last moments I had with my mom were spent fighting. I was filled with shame and regret about what I had said to her. This sent me deeper down into the pit. I felt it wasn't fair that she had to die and I had to be the one to live. I was the family screw up and here I was still alive. I didn't think it was fair that I got to watch my niece and nephew grow up and she missed it all. It wasn't fair.

I tried to run from everything and everyone and ended up running to Ohio. My depression quickly led to drinking. I found my comfort in a bottle. Yet despite my drinking, my depression and suicidal thoughts were still there. At times, they were so intense I could barely function. No matter what I did, I couldn't escape them. I considered getting help at one point in time, but felt that asking for help was admitting I was too weak to handle things. I then left my job to pursue another one.

The new job was a bit more stressful and only added to my depression. Things were so out of control with my emotions and my thoughts. It was then that I realized that maybe I should get some help. I surrendered to my weakness. I explored an online counseling service and it was there I began online counseling with Kristie.

The counseling helped alleviate some of the depression but I still struggled with my suicidal thoughts daily. I also then began seeing a psychiatrist who started me on a started a daily medication regiment to help alleviate the intensity of my emotions and thoughts.

Despite the medication and counseling, I had a moment of utter weakness. I hit one of my lowest points. I had lost all hope and the will to survive. I had decided that this would be the day I end all this pain that I had struggled with for so many years. I wrote a few letters to some friends to say goodbye and then took some pills that I had in my apartment. I don't remember much after that, but I woke up in the hospital. Apparently, a friend found me and took me there. I was angry that I was still alive. I began to think that my parents were right and that I could do nothing right. I couldn't even be successful at ending my own life. It was very frustrating.

I was then evaluated by a hospital psychiatrist and basically told them what they needed to hear. I just wanted to get out of the hospital. A few days later I was discharged. I resumed my counseling and medication regiment. It was going well and I was gaining control of my emotions and thoughts. I learned new skills to deal with my feelings. I grew stronger through all of it. I learned resilience and to not give up on life. I realized that there is a reason for me to be here on this earth.

The biggest thing I wish people understood about depression is that those who suffer from it aren't outcasts. We are human, just like they are. We also aren't broken beyond repair. We are just like them but are struggling a bit more. We feel things more intensely and that is also one of the things that makes us struggle more.

People who feel that suicide is the only answer have lost hope. They also just want to end the pain they have been struggling with for so long. I know that for me, I just wanted to end the pain that had weighed me down for so many years. I didn't see a purpose for my life and I believed this world would be better off without me, but that wasn't the case. Suicide seemed like the only way to escape all of it.

In my road to recovery, I have found that a regiment of medication has been helpful. I also go to counseling on a regular basis and am continuing to work on the skills I have learned to help deal with my emotions and thoughts. I have also learned that seeking help wasn't a sign of weakness but a sign of strength. I still have some rough days, but they can't compare to how things use to be before I sought out help. I am still a work in progress and look forward to continuing to heal as I walk through this. I know I will ultimately overcome this.

To those who feel that suicide is the only answer, it's not. There is hope, and always a reason to live. You may not see it now through the pain, but you will one day. The biggest thing is to seek out help. There are people who truly care about you. I care about you. Seeking out help isn't a sign of weakness, but rather it is a sign of great strength. If you have never struggled with depression and thoughts of suicide, it's hard to understand what we go through. Take the time to let the person you know that is struggling that you truly care. Most importantly, just be there and listen. You don't need to say a thing, just be a friend and listen.

The verse that always echoes in my mind is Jeremiah 29:13. You will seek me and find me when you seek with all your heart. I need to be constantly seeking God and his will for my life. It is only then I will have hope and a purpose. It is only through seeking his will that I will *rise!*

Something cosmic is occurring

So much bigger than you and I

It's beyond that glance

The look in your eye

Something beautiful is happening

Right there inside of you

It's a transformation of spirit

Can you feel it in what you do?

Something new is on the horizon

Something so wild and free

The journey begins with just one step

Each day, just let it be

Something magical is coming

If you believe inside your soul

Release your inner demons

Allow your light to glow

Something lost will be found

An unexpected twist

Don't force anything

Simply follow your bliss

Something cosmic is occurring

Something wonderful is beginning...

-Jessica D. Comer

Chapter 24

Tears of Cleansing

by Joe Ciz

My name is Joseph. I am from Mars. I am a heavy equipment mechanic. I have 3 children. I have wanted to share my story for such a long time but I didn't have the opportunity, or a person to share it with. Through this book project I am ready to share it. I want to help others. If my story can save a life, then it is worth it. I am finally ok with myself.

It was around the age of 13 that I noticed I wasn't myself. I was sad all the time. Depressed. I didn't have any energy either. I was tired all the time. I did not want to spend time with my friends, family, or do the things that I used to like to do.

I wish I could say I told someone. I wish I could say I asked for help. I didn't. I didn't know what to do. I was embarrassed that I was having suicidal thoughts. I was embarrassed by what I was feeling, you know, weak. Like someone who couldn't handle life and I thought that made me weak. It just wasn't talked about much. Even now people don't like to talk about it. It's just wrong;

that's another reason why I want to tell my story. I want people to know it is okay to tell. It is okay to get help. They are not alone.

Around the age of 17 my thoughts got worse. I was no longer just sad. I thought about killing myself all the time. Relationships are hard you know. I was hurt by a girl. She had cheated on me. I felt so betrayed and alone. She was the first girl I trusted. I couldn't understand what I had done wrong. I didn't want to live anymore.

It's really hard to talk about my suicide attempt. There were a few times. I will just share one now.

It was because this girl hurt me. I had a gun. I do not remember what the day was like but, I just got into a very dark place. I was at my parents' house. I was outside. I was going to shoot myself but I couldn't do it. I knew it just wasn't my time to die even though the pain was too much. I also didn't want to be a great disappointment. I knew my family would be really hurt. I couldn't do that to them. I just sat a cried. I was heartbroken.

I want people to know that there is always someone that will listen. Or talk to. That is how I was able to work through it. I talked to someone and I kept my favorite quote from Palms 23 in my mind. I even had it tattooed on my leg to remind me.

I would say to others that it is selfish. I do not know how to explain it; it will cause more problems for everyone around you. Everybody has some kind of demon in them. You cannot keep it bottled up.

Chapter 25

The Final Dance

by Anonymous

"There is a surrendering to your story and then a knowing that you don't have to stay in your story."

- Collete Baron Reid

My story doesn't begin or end with suicide. I'm still here and so are you. I'm 35 years old. I grew up on Long Island, NY. I went to school for ballet and psychology. I have worked with teenagers in the mental field for about ten years. If I help to save one life or shift a single person's perspective, then sharing my story is worth it. My intention is not to hurt or offend anyone in the sharing of my story.

My faith has gotten me through the darkest days, along with my unique perspective on life. I could share the trauma I have experienced in life but I would rather focus on how I lived through it, how I survived. It is my hope that my choice to not share details wont diminish the impact of my story. I trust I won't be judged nor will readers feel my trauma must have been less intense to get through. I hope you the reader can understand that each person's trauma is uniquely experienced by them and cannot be compared or judged as less than or greater than another's authentic experience.

Difficult times for me started at a very young age, 6 years old. As a kid, there were a lot of gray areas --there were wonderful days and there were horrible days. I mean, it was my life. It was status quo. It was how it was, I didn't know anything different. I would feel physically sick a lot and I would miss school. I think what I went through physically affected me a lot. I have to say, I never really had thoughts of harming myself. I did go to bed praying that God would just take me in my sleep, that I just wouldn't wake up. Because of my relationship with God and my church, it never entered my mind to physically hurt myself or take my own life. I was also scared as a kid, always seeking to make others happy. I feel my thinking was if everyone around me was happy then bad things wouldn't happen. I was definitely a people pleaser. Inside I was sad, depressed, scared, and often felt physically sick.

I really found comfort and support through things that I loved. I did ballet and danced 4 or 5 nights a week. I was head of my youth group and either lived at dance class or church or school for the most part. Church was like my family, my home. I found a lot of comfort in those places and those activities and the people I was around. At some point in high school I started talking about it, I felt like I had more control over myself and my thoughts and where my life was going to go. I didn't talk about it necessarily because I felt like I needed help, I talked about it because I felt empowered talking about it. By owning it and saying this happened to me, it didn't have power of me anymore. It was a part of what had happened to me but it wasn't who I was. I realized somehow at a young age that I could have control over my life and who I was going to be. As I stated previously I went on to get a degree in psychology and work with suicidal teens. We have a saying we teach them; recognize it, name it, then tell it what to do. If you can't look at it and own what happened, it is hard to tell it what to do- hard to push out the negative and be open to the future, all the positive possibilities and goals for your future.

The biggest thing for me, that I shared with teens working in mental health, is that when bad things happen to you that you can't control (especially as a child), you can't continue to allow that to rule your life as you get older or time goes on. Don't say this happened to me so this is why I am how I am or why I'm upset or why I am angry or why I can't achieve things or do this or that. I feel like you are victimizing yourself. I think a big way of my thinking was "Yes, this happened to me I had no control over it and I was a victim but this person/these circumstances they are not here anymore. If I continue to look at it that way, I'm victimizing myself."

What was I going to do, who did I want to be? Taking responsibility for my life and my actions and living each day, actively living in the moment was empowering for me. I found it to be very powerful with teenagers that I work with as well. Even with things they were going through in their lives they didn't have power over, I would as them "Who do you want to be, 'cause in ten years when this is not your life anymore, you're going to be responsible for you and what does that look like?" They realize they can either give this person power over them, have a horrible day and think about all these negative things, or they can choose to have power over their own thoughts and their own day.

When you've gone through something where you have felt so out of control, it is really empowering to take that control back, to see you have a choice. That's where I have seen the shift in the teenagers I work with, when they get that.

I worked with teenagers that have either attempted suicide and been in the hospital or were having really strong thoughts to do so. They had all different kinds of backgrounds: abuse, anxiety, eating disorders, mostly mood kinds of things. They all had their different stories, different family settings, school pressures. I did a lot of skill teaching, cognitive behavioral therapy, mindfulness.

It became really apparent that these are skills that everybody can benefit from in life and that one of the biggest ones was radical acceptance and being able to accept things how they are and not how you want them to be. You can get so upset over how you feel things should be or how you want them to be instead of accepting how they are, what you can and can't control. I can say that is something I struggled with throughout my life and something that by working with these kids and teaching these skills I have learned. You can't teach this every day and not live that way, it becomes a big struggle and looking at what you can control compared to the little things that aren't yours –don't take on someone else's issues you have no control over or the things or the things that are going on you can't change. If you focus on the things you can control and let go of the stuff that's not yours it makes it easier to get through your day.

I don't know where my resilience came from but I thank God for it. When I first started working with suicidal teens I often went home and cried wondering how I got through without harming myself as I saw so many teens cutting and attempting suicide. If you are struggling find someone to talk to, someone you trust, somewhere safe. Make sure you focus on the things you love and who you want to be because your life is not over and you have a lot of life to live. You get to choose how you do it. Remember: this too shall pass. I know it's cliché, a lot of people use it, but it is so true when it comes to feelings and thoughts. Yes, it sucks, whatever you're feeling right now sucks, but at the same time it is going to pass, you're going to feel differently in an hour, a day, a week, and that even when you're feeling happy it is going to pass. Happiness is feeling not a destination.

Readers be mindful that everyone's journey is different. Be mindful of how you speak to people, know that they could be struggling right now and the things you say and do affect the people around you. Be kind. When people are angry and unkind is often when they need your love and kindness the most.

"Everything can be taken from a man but one thing: the last of the human freedoms – to choose one's attitude in any given set of circumstances, to choose one's own way."

– Viktor Frankl

Chapter 26

I am Redeemed

by Gary Griggs

I was born in Washington DC. My mom was Italian and my dad was American. They came from good backgrounds but they grew up during the depression. My father's family was really poor.

When my father was 17 years old, his dad died in a car accident. Being the oldest of five children, he had to take care of them and his mother. My father was a really intelligent man who ended up working in the White House for a while, and then as an airline executive. He started his own company and I was born in 1964.

I was an only child. An older brother died 7 days after his birth. I had a really great childhood because my parents loved me deeply. As I grew older, my father wanted so much for me but he had a problem with putting me down. If I did something to make him angry, he would say if I kept doing what I was doing, I was never going to amount to anything. His words cut deep because the only thing I was trying to do was please him. That's when the emotional scarring began and I started getting that chip on my shoulder.

Although he was a genuine, loving person, the problem was the way he expressed his love. I used to be ashamed of my life because I came from a really good background and had good morals. I was taught honesty, love, and respect for others. We lived in a blue-collar neighborhood. However, my father became really successful, and overnight we went from blue-collar straight to living in a mansion. I was this new kid on the block, trying to fit in.

I started getting into drugs in 7th grade because it seemed like the thing to do at the time. Weed was everywhere. When I smoked weed the first time, it was the best experience of my whole life because it took me out of something, I didn't feel pain any more. That's when I started getting into drugs. I do believe we are predisposed to addiction and I think I have that gene. After the marijuana, I got into LSD, and then PCP. My grades began dropping and my dad started feeling like he was losing control of me. Once I knew that, I had him wrapped around my finger. I learned manipulation at an early age, working my parents against one another. I dropped out of school at 16 to work for my dad. He had a huge million-dollar company and my dream was to run that company someday. The problem was I never learned responsibility. I started getting out of control at that point and my mom was always worried sick.

The suicidal thoughts didn't occur until many years later. I learned how to manipulate the court system at an early age. My parents had me locked up when I was a juvenile because they thought it would teach me a lesson. It was a horrible experience, but it taught me how to survive in that situation. One of the judges ordered my father and I to go to counseling. It was the first time we even thought about going to counseling. I didn't think I had a problem, and my dad was the type who didn't believe in mental health problems. We went to the appointment because the judge ordered us to go. I started getting into heroin, and amphetamines. The reason I didn't see my problems was because my parents were such big enablers. I had a safety net if anything went wrong. I would come home and the problem would blow over. Finally, my father stopped paying for lawyers and paying for me to get out of jail. I ended up doing time.

A major trauma in my life was my mom died in 1997 from cancer. When she died, that took a big chunk out of my dad and I. He blamed me for her death which made me feel even shittier.

In 2001, my drug addiction escalated and was out of control. I was into cocaine at this point and still living at home. My father's close friends said, "Wayne, you're going to have to separate and move and don't tell him." And that's what happened. One day he called me home and said, "I'm selling the house. I'm moving and I'm not sure where I'm going." He asked me how much money I needed to get it together. All I was thinking about was getting high, so I told him a couple thousand dollars. He gave me the money and I ended up getting high. I came back to get more money. When I arrived, six of his friends were moving all of his stuff. They hired a bodyguard service to be at the house. I asked to talk to my dad and was told he didn't want to see me. That was the last I saw of him.

For 2 weeks after he moved out, I kept going back to the house because I couldn't believe that he was gone. That's when the depression started coming in hard and thoughts of suicide. I ended up on the streets of Baltimore, on parole and on the run. I was 35 or 40, and that's when I got the gun. I was living in abandoned houses and shooting dope. I did some dope one day and I decided I should do it. I was scared. I had to get really high to do it, because I had always been scared of dying. I never wanted to die. I loved life. That's what was so confusing. When I pulled the trigger, the gun jammed. I thought, *I can't even do that right.* They ended up catching me in Baltimore on the run and locked me up. When you violate parole, they automatically put a warrant out for your arrest. The parole board then decides whether you go back to prison to finish the rest of your sentence. There's always a different parole commissioner every two weeks. When my day came, I had the worst one possible.

When I was the holding section, I said this prayer, "God if you can hear me right now, please, I don't want to go back to prison because that's not what I need. I want to change my life. Please help." I went into the hearing and the parole commissioner asked me why I hadn't followed up on any of my parole visits. I told him that I had been in and out of prison and I didn't want that life anymore and if he could find it in his heart to give me another chance I wouldn't let him down. He responded, "I don't even really know why I'm doing this. But there is something that is compelling me to do it. Mr. Griggs, I'm going to release you today." I was the only one out of 50 people that he released.

So I went back to Maryland. It was wintertime. A kind nurse let me sleep in a hospital lobby until Sunday morning. I walked to a little drug store on the corner. As I was standing there I said, "God, I don't know which direction to go, please help me." As soon as I said that a car came flying into the parking lot and a guy got out of the car, walked up to me and asked if I was homeless. I said I was and he told me to wait a minute. He had to get a prescription for his wife. He came out of the store and he told me to get in his car. I was really on guard at this point.

His name was Vince. He had a PhD and was a doctor with his own practice in town. He did mental health assessments for the sheriff and police departments. He was looking for someone to care for his wife who had MS. She needed help her with meds, to cook, and clean. I told him I would love to do that. His wife was looking at him. I was so scared and I was scared for her. I didn't want her to freak out because I wasn't a bad person. Vince explained that by running into me, God had answered his prayers. His wife asked to speak with him privately. I was in the other room, hearing bits and pieces. She asked Vince if he was crazy, since I had just been released from prison. When they called me back in the living room, they asked for my social security number to do a background check. She asked me to tell her what I had done and I was totally honest.

Since I had never hurt anybody and never had any violent crimes, she agreed to the arrangement. She was a professional artist and I was an artist too. She also taught art and had a PhD. She had this huge studio that Vince built for her, with a sunroom, tons of canvas and paint and she told me I was welcome to go in there anytime. It was incredible. I spent a year there taking care of her.

She couldn't do anything. It was a humbling experience because of where I came from. They offered their van for me to use. So I started going to meetings and then Vince would come talk to me. What I liked about him was he was a psychiatrist but he never acted like one at home. He would talk to me but it was like as a friend; he wasn't there to diagnose me.

That was the major turning point for me in deciding to change my life; when I started seeking professional help because I knew I had depression and anxiety. I was diagnosed with ADHD and anxiety. Initially, I was scared to write this story. But, I want others to be aware how your life can be great. It's easy to get to a point where you don't care anymore. Yet, there are so many positive things to live for

When you make a decision to not feel like crap all the time, you start to find things that replace the bad. I've learned through the years from being in and out of recovery, what works for me. I've been through the really bad and worked out of it without somebody helping me and I found ways to cope through things without medication. I hate medication. It makes me feel like crap. I've hospitalized myself 3 times. Also, God is a big component. I know God's there. What I want people to know is if you're feeling this, to give yourself a moment to reflect on the good stuff and pull out of the spiral.

I wish people would understand depression and suicide. People are close-minded. They live in bubbles. They don't want to see the bad. I think people look at mental illness as bad and it's not, it's just like any other medical condition. It's been a stigma that's been ingrained in people. People get diseases all the time and they're accepted. So why wouldn't you accept somebody who's going through an emotional crisis? It's just a different part of the body. One day I'd like to talk to people. Because when I talk and tell you an experience, you feel it, it really comes from the heart. I'm an artist, a chef. I have many beautiful gifts that God's given me. My mom always told me, "God's got something really wonderful planned for you." I just don't know what it is yet.

For me, the Bible is key. I know God's in my heart and when I speak I say what's on my heart. I'm not ashamed of anything. I've accepted my past. If nobody else can accept it that's on them. What keeps me going is God. He lives inside me and I know that now. I never had that closeness, even though my parents raised me as Christian. My mom tried to instill God into my heart and I just blew her off. But that's what saved my life, even though I didn't follow God at the time, he saved my life. If I can help someone then I want to help someone. That's what God is putting on my heart now.

Chapter 27

A River Turning Red

by Anonymous

Healing comes when we shine light into dark places. In sharing my story, I want to bring hope to others, by letting them know there is light at the end of the tunnel. As I notice more children having anxious moments, my hope is that by openly talking about the daily challenges, including different ways we can work through them, we will be able to stop suicide from being thought of as an option.

Growing up, we didn't talk about our feelings in our family. My mom was in and out of the hospital for mental illness frequently during my school age years. It wasn't talked about openly back then, not even within our family. I grew to become an anxious child without a good understanding of how to cope.

While my mom was out of the house, I was sexually abused as a child. This put me in a downward spiral of thinking that I was no good, and at one point I even felt like I was possessed by demons. I remember having one specific dream of a man in a white suit coming out of clouds on a white horse to take me away. That dream scared me something awful. Much later in life I realized that was our savior coming down to protect me from what was happening to me here on earth.

Sunday nights became rough – the tensions of the week built up and let go in a well of tears. During high school, my parents got divorced. It was good for them to separate, but that put more stress and pressure on me as I became more responsible for the household. During that time, I felt unseen. No one was sticking up for me. The pressure just became too overwhelming. I wanted to disappear, to become invisible and escape. I didn't think of it as being suicidal, but that's what it was. I didn't want to 'die.' I just wanted to disappear from the pain. I had developed an eating disorder and my weight dropped significantly. I was blacking out some days at school and having major headaches. I didn't specifically reach out to anyone. Thankfully there was a caring teacher, our A.P. chemistry teacher, who would give me a bottle of seltzer water during class. Her actions were enough to let me know that someone cared about me. During that same year, in English class, I wrote a poem:

My heart is crying tears of black,

Flowing from a river,

A river turning red.

The English teacher said whoever wrote that poem should just kill themselves. Maybe that woke me up out of falling into a pit of darkness. By the time I graduated high school, I was back to a normal weight and feeling optimistic about the future. Realizing that me disappearing from this earth would not hurt the people who hurt me helped me move forward in recovery. In fact, they would have won, by me being obliterated from the face of the earth.

For college, I moved out of state. This gave me a chance to make a fresh start with people who had no prior expectation of who I was. It allowed me to explore and re-invent myself in a positive light. I gave myself permission to explore things that gave me joy – some as simple as coloring in coloring books, others more complex like performing in a modern dance group. It wasn't until years later that I sought out a counselor to work with, and that is the one thing that would have helped if I did it earlier. I highly recommend taking that step sooner rather than later for anyone who may be struggling. Thankfully I have a very supportive husband, who soon after we were married showed me full support in getting whatever help I needed.

Today I choose to surround myself with positive people. Not just happy go lucky people, but people who are open in sharing their struggles and kind enough to not be judgmental when you share yours. I still have my moments when I feel down, but I can honestly say that I haven't felt like committing suicide in a long time. I try to focus my heart and mind on gratitude, and remind myself that falling down and getting back up again is just another part of the road to success.

What I want others to understand about suicide:

If a person has experienced suicide in their family, even an attempted suicide, it may seem like a viable option to them.

It is ok to ask questions if you suspect someone is struggling with suicidal thoughts – Are you thinking about committing suicide? How can I help you get through today?

If you find yourself in a dark place contemplating suicide, have faith – knowing God was there for me, when I felt that no one else was, got me through some really rough times. Also, be open to reaching out to friends whose beliefs are in line with yours. Friends are there to lift each other up, and you never know, they may have been in a dark place themselves once.

If you've never struggled with depression, anxiety, or thoughts of suicide, count yourself as blessed! You have a unique perspective to share with someone who may be struggling. They may turn to you for help. Acknowledge their feelings, and let them know that there is life after the struggle. Let them know that while you've never felt as they do, that you too have struggles that take some time to work through. Part of being human is experiencing the joys, sadness, frustrations, elations. Without feeling the lows, we wouldn't appreciate the high points as much.

There is a joy you experience after you move beyond thoughts of suicide. You are strong. You are fierce. You have made the decision to live your own life, and no one can take that away from you. You can step up and help another person who may attempt suicide. Just be open to that possibility. God brings you through these challenges for good – trust me, I know, because I am living it.

31 Put aside all bitterness, losing your temper, anger, shouting, and slander, along with every other evil. 32 Be kind, compassionate, and forgiving to each other, in the same way God forgave you in Christ.

- Ephesians 4:31-32

19 When my anxious thoughts multiply within me, your consolations delight my soul.

- Psalm 94:19

Chapter 28

The God of Second Chances
by Paula Miles

"...the King is enthralled by your beauty; honor Him, for He is your Lord."

Psalm 45:11 (NIV)

When I was growing up, the word, "suicide" was usually whispered under quiet breaths. The misunderstanding and stigma so strong, people who 'did that' were assumed to be hell bound. The words "mentally ill" conjured up images of people in straitjackets. As a child and adolescent, the thought of taking my own life was never on my radar. But, once the teen years hit, the toll of living in a household with copious amounts of conflict began to crack the wall I had carefully built around myself to keep out the pain.

Looking back, I am certain this is when the depression began. It was also the time I first considered suicide. I had reached a place where I thought if I wasn't around, my parents could divorce and be happy. Being lost in the idea that somehow the world would be better off without you, creates a powerful vortex of despair. I can still remember making a phone call to my best friend. I wanted to say goodbye and tell her I loved her. Clearly, there was still a part of me that wanted to live because I reached out.

We talked, she threatened to call my parents or tell her parents. She refused to let me off the phone. I say that, but of course, all I had to do was hang up the phone (we are talking late 70's here). However, I never hung up until she was certain she had talked me out of my plan. The funny thing is I didn't actually have a plan. I just figured I would slit my wrists after my parents fell asleep. Guns weren't accessible and there wasn't a good place to hang a rope. Between this first foray in suicidal thoughts and my high school graduation day, I would make 2 other similar calls to my friend. I have no way of knowing what would have happened had she not been home, but I am firmly convinced she saved my life.

I carried my buried sadness to college. In retrospect, I didn't understand or even know about depression. Often, I would play my guitar in moments of 'blueness' and grow introspective, but being a creative soul, I knew deep emotions were part of the territory.

It was in my junior year of college that suicidal thoughts once again attacked. I was dating a beautiful soul of a man for a couple months. We clicked on so many levels. He was ruggedly handsome, muscular, athletic, creative, and respectful. We enjoyed walks and talked about our faith. He would play his guitar or the piano for me. He had been recruited for diving and was as much of an artist off the board as he was when he danced across the stage. I fell hard for him.

Things were different in the early 80's. Homosexuality or bisexuality were just beginning to be heard on college campuses. There was such a stereotype back then and he didn't fit the stereotype at all. In my naiveté, I was blind until a friend on my dorm floor pulled me aside one day. She gently informed me the man I had fallen in love with was struggling with his sexual identity. While she had given him the opportunity to tell me himself, he was too scared. I was beyond shattered. When confronted, he admitted I had confused him. He was attracted to me. I gave him two weeks to decide between me and the guy he had been seeing at the same time we were dating. Ultimately, at the end of those two weeks, he rejected me and everything I felt as a woman was destroyed; he had chosen a man over me. I remember running from campus all the way out to a cemetery on the edge of town. I sobbed until I had no more tears left in me. My deep heart pain was so acute. I had grabbed a butter knife from my dorm room before I left. I ran it through my hands for a long time, contemplating the mess of my life; contemplating the end of my life. I prayed and he was able to break through and remind me of the devastation my parents and family would feel. Although I felt worthless, the pattern of putting others before myself proved to be the thing that saved my life that day.

Thirty-four years have passed since that awful day. There have been times of fleeting suicidal thoughts. But, two years ago, almost to the date of writing this chapter, I was sitting in a mall parking lot, alone, on a Sunday afternoon, as a slight drizzle fell on the car. It felt like the darkest period of my life. My marriage of 29 years was splintered. In spite of counseling, we took three steps back for every two forward. I had lived in denial of the verbal abuse that occurred through the marriage. Our daughter was living with anxiety and depression rooted in the angry home environment in which she grew, making choices for which I held myself responsible. There were personal demons that caused me to be demanding of attention and constant affirmation in some friendships. Because of the emotional detachment I felt in my marriage, I tried to fill that void in other people. I had a beautiful friend who struggled to trust female friendships. She had been wounded and abandoned too many times, but I was going to be the one who helped her open up, trust, and feel safe. And I did…until my demons reared. Without consultation, I told my friend she no longer needed me in her life. My words and actions pierced her soul as I threw her trust back into the hands from which she had given it. Only when it was too late to retrieve words, did I finally understand the childhood wounds that caused me to act as I did. No apology, no explanation could delete my words. I sat in my car, drowning in my grief at a friendship lost, the emptiness in my marriage, and a complete sense of failing the beautiful daughter who was my heart.

I broke, wanting the searing pain to stop. Death seemed a welcome answer. The anxiety was closing in and I was struggling to gain air. I was so scared, knowing I was at critical mass. I sent a text to my therapist, who was also a friend. There was no expectation of forgiveness, I simply needed direction. *Who should I call? I'm scared? The pain is too much. There is no legacy but hurt and failure. Even though I have no right to ask, promise me you'll take care of my girl's heart.*

Unlike any other time, my method of suicide was clear. I would turn my car from the gray parking lot, head towards the interstate, hit the accelerator, and drive it straight into the first concrete object I found. Then, it would all be over. I was strangely at peace. I prayed, pouring out my heart and telling Jesus I was coming home soon. I asked his forgiveness for not being strong enough, for not trusting enough, for hurting so many. Only one thing was stopping me. My therapist kept texting me. This deeply wounded friend was setting aside her pain to try and 'talk me down.' I hated and loved her all at the same time. Why wouldn't she leave me alone to die? She kept reminding me how much my daughter still needed me, that it wasn't fair to her, even if she was 17. She appealed to my faith. Somewhere deep inside, rational began to overtake emotion; weakness turned to fragile strength and God's spirit ministered in the cloudy thoughts. I didn't leave the parking lot until I was certain I would live. I held no illusions that suddenly my marriage would be perfect or my daughter's wounds healed. There was a resignation that I had destroyed a friendship. In fact, everything was still the same as when I pulled the car into that lot. But, I was not the same. Once you've teetered on the precipice of no return and found your balance, you can face another day.

Two years later, my marriage has moved mostly forward. Our beautiful daughter is thriving as a sophomore in college. The friendship I thought I had destroyed…God had an incredible restoration project planned that leaves me thankful every day that he is a healing God.

My prayer as you read this chapter is to understand it is not a natural emotion to want to die. The natural emotion is a desire to avoid pain. Every time I faced the thoughts and came so very close the last time, was for one reason…I simply did not want to feel pain anymore. Pain that leads to suicidal thoughts is an all-encompassing, suffocating existence. The darkness feels impenetrable. However, I had to be reminded that I would be inflicting the same pain I was trying to escape. How could I leave that legacy? The hardest step is to reach out. But, it's the only way to live.

Chapter 29

Voices and Choices

by Abigail Miles

"The hardest thing in the world is to live in it. Be brave. Live."

–Buffy Summers

I can't remember a time when I wasn't sad. My earliest memories include an anger at myself for being alive, and a jealousy to all those children that had died when they were young. My outlook on death was positive; too positive. I longed for death more than I did for life. I found life tiresome and even at a young age, I understood that a moment basking in the glory of God in eternity would be better than one's whole life. I wanted it. I craved it.

This want was stemmed out of a multitude of things. My brain, fiercely logical and rational, went systematically through the benefits of life and finding death or being with God, more fulfilling.

My genetics, from which I received the both depression (from my mother) and anxiety (from my father). My circumstances, with an angry, mentally abusive father and a terrible home dynamic. My clinical depression and anxiety, combined with my unfailing logic, and a terrible home, made the thought of death slowly fester and over many years it became an integral part of my brain development. When one is so young and thinking these thoughts, it becomes part of the brain as they grow. It becomes a coping mechanism that is completely ingrained into the brain and how it thinks. Literally, suicide is written into the brain's programming. Because I was so little, this happened to me. I am still feeling its effects, as my brain tends to fail back on this coping mechanism still. I'm not suicidal; but my brain and its wiring *wants* me to be. Therefore, it's a constant battle when things get tough. I recognize it now and am able to combat it, but as I was growing up, I had no idea what was going on. And therefore, I was very suicidal.

The one tool God had given me to fight this integral part of me was another integral part of me. I was logical and rational and with those two traits came a very strong sense of right and wrong. I knew the consequences of my actions should I choose to act on this. There was no going back from this. I knew, beyond a shadow of a doubt, that if I chose to go through with this path I would not be saved. There would be no saving in the nick of time, I would die. Period. I can't exactly say how I knew this, but I did. This idea stopped me, the idea of making a permanent decision. Because of my father, I had extreme commitment issues and in a very twisted way, his anger saved me. The commitment issues ultimately were higher and scarier than the longing to die. But the fight was long. Each time it was tedious.

My first true attempt came when I was twelve or thirteen, I can't quite remember which. I had just come back from a church retreat and that anxiety nightmare, coupled with the fact I had spent an entire weekend surrounded by a toxic, selfish friend left me rundown and simply tired. I was tired of the fight against my (then unknown) depression and anxiety and tired of simply never wanting to have been born. I wanted to die. I wanted to be free of the struggles of this life and free of the ones to come. My life had felt like a constant uphill battle from the time I was consciously aware and I was so sick of it. I felt broken. I sat in my room, a candle in front of me, a steak knife pressed against my heart (perhaps not the most effective way, but I was determined to die in a similar way to those who believed this way was an honorable death. It was a justification for myself and a pride one too). I sobbed. I tried to text this toxic friend, but she never responded. She never did. My instincts fought each other, one wanting to die and the other stubborn part of me wanting to live just to say, "I lived. I made it. Screw all of you, *I made it.*" As I fought, a song came on the radio I had turned on. It was JJ Heller's 'What Love Really Means.' It really got to me, I was so lost, tired, and lonely that I cried out to God. Then I put the knife down, I blew out the candle, and I repeated one line of that song, "Oh Lord, forgive me, I want to go home." Over and over again. And I prayed, with all my heart, that I would not wake up the next morning. As I drifted in and out of consciousness, I felt a peace come over me. Complete peace. I felt a breeze blow through, one that felt cool and told of springtime and happiness. I heard, in my exhausted and slightly delirious state, an old voice, deep, and kind say to me, "You will live to see these days renewed, my beautiful daughter." I fell into a sleep that was so dreamless and so restful, I have not slept as peacefully since.

This should be the end of the story. I should have went flying into a field of daises singing Justin Bieber songs and everything should have been perfect.

Everything was not perfect.

The toxic friend and I got closer. We became desperately dependent on one another and anyone who knows what healthy relationships are knows that this is *not it.* In trying to keep her and another boy I had met alive and hopeful, I began to sink. I was not healthy myself and keeping them alive took everything out of me. They couldn't handle my problems since theirs were just so horrible that they were on the edge of a knife constantly. My problems weren't *big* enough or *important* enough for them to take notice. I was an amazing actress, trying to keep myself alive while also trying to pull those two out of the darkness. I wanted to save them, I had to save them. If I could save them, I could save myself. There's a line in Buffy the Vampire Slayer that talks about how you reach into the abyss to pull someone out and then they drop in further. So you reach further and further and before you know it, you're in with them. You try and lead them out, because that means you know the way out. But there is no way out, not with them anyway. I learned, painfully and over many years, you can't save *anyone.* Nor is it your job to save anyone. If you think that is your calling in life, you need to take a serious look at yourself.

These people, combined with the terrible things they were mixed up in, wore on me. I had numerous attempts at suicide, each time fighting myself enough to put the knife or pills down. Every time I would call these people. Often, they ignored me or were too high or drunk to pick up my calls. They would talk to me maybe three months out of the year. It became a pattern, one that wore on me and my self-esteem. I felt lonely and lost. The two people who I thought understood me the most couldn't even bother to make time to send me a text. It was because of this low self-esteem I got into a bad relationship with a person who eventually sexually assaulted me. After that, I was completely beaten. I had the pills in my mouth. It took everything in me to defy what had happened to me and to spit them out.

I spit the pills out.

This constant act of defiance made me strong. This stubbornness to not die was what made me strong. It wasn't that I didn't have to strength to die; it was that God gave me the strength to *choose* not to. I had to make a choice, every time, to live or to die. I had to choose to live or to die. I had to *choose*.

The hardest parts of our lives often occur when we think we don't have a choice. The demons are great at making us feel like we don't have a choice. There is *always* a choice. One is just more difficult than the other. This is your freedom of being human, is to choose. Don't let your demons take away your voice. Your scream is louder than their voices and there is power in that.

I began to talk. I began to open up to my counselor. I chose to begin to heal myself. I had to make the first step. The hardest part was relying on other people, people like my counselor, to help fix me. I am still working on the fixing part. I don't think that part will ever end, but the fact that I chose this path, to make myself better, put the power back in my hands. I am beautiful in my painful story. I am beautiful. And so are you. Don't let fear stop you from making your choice and getting your voice back. You deserve to *live*.

"The greatest risk any of us will ever take-to be seen as we truly are."

– Cinderella, 2015

Chapter 30

Surviving Myself

by Sabrina Philips

Life is what you make it, right? Well I managed to make mine a big old mess! This was not supposed to be my life. Where did I go wrong? I was 35. I was supposed to be married and settled with a big, beautiful home and a fabulous career! I certainly was not meant to be a single mother of two, going through yet another break up, facing eviction and killing myself at a serving job. Yet there I was.

Don't get me wrong, my children are the greatest gift I have ever received, and I loved my job, boss, and coworkers. This, however, was not what I wanted the rest of my life to look like. Every day, I was falling deeper and deeper into the dark hole of my depression. I didn't even know myself anymore!

I began working nonstop to escape my reality and to make sure my children and I were not homeless. I had lost my license due to a DUI and was literally begging for rides to and from work daily. I felt like such a pathetic loser. I hated my life and how awful it had become. I had always been so independent, so having to ask for help felt like it physically hurt.

I hated that I had become such a disappointment to everyone important in my life, especially my daughters. I began drinking and abusing my prescription Xanax. A lot. I cut off friends and family because I didn't want them to see how worthless I felt I had become.

Soon, I was drinking daily to escape the reality of being me. This, of course, made everything so much worse. My daughters no longer wanted to be around me and I was screwing up badly at work. I decided my girl's lives would be so much better without a horrible mother like me.

I locked myself in the bathroom, ran myself a bath, and washed down all the pills I had with some bathroom cleaner. At least that's what I tried to do. I was such a wreck, I even failed at killing myself. I just became incredibly sick. I know now that it was God's plan for me to live.

I decided that I wanted to live, and be the mother my baby girls deserved. I still had to figure out a way to get myself out of the hole I had pretty much thrown myself down. It may sound insane, but getting arrested saved my life. I got picked up for not completing the requirements for my D.U.I. During the 38 days of my incarceration, I found God, my motivation and determination, and most importantly, myself.

I had nothing but time to think about how and why my life got so out of control and what I was going to do to fix it. I was able to talk to my friends, family, and daughters with a clear mind. I was also able to make a plan for when I got out. I gained a new determination to make the best of the rest of my life.

I came home ready for a completely fresh start, shaved head and all. I had a lot of work ahead of me, though. When I got out, I found that I had lost my job, apartment, and my oldest daughter had moved in with my mother. The old me would have let this break me, but not the new and improved me. The new me was ready to use this second chance to the fullest.

My youngest and I packed a few bags and started our journey to our new and improved life. In two short months, I have found a job, a new apartment, joined a new church, and enrolled in community college. I have also started in outpatient rehab. As I write, I am 53 days sober. I couldn't have done any of this without the incredible support of my friends and family, my church, and the amazing programs offered in my community.

Every day just keeps getting better and I am so blessed to still be alive to see it. I am grateful that my attempt to end my life was unsuccessful and for what I have learned from it. Now, I get to fix my past mistakes and watch my little girls grow up. Hopefully one day I can make them as proud of me as I am of them. I have definitely had a few dark chapters in my story so far, but I am so excited to see what wonderful adventures the rest of my story holds. I am a proud survivor of myself.

To anyone out there feeling lost or alone or worthless, know that you are loved. You are important. There are so many adventures out there for you! Please don't give up! Reach out and let someone know how you are feeling. Your story isn't over yet. Make it incredible.

Chapter 31

Coming Back from the Dark

by Claire Snow-Downing

In the summer of 2010 I was diagnosed with post-traumatic stress disorder, six years after my daughter's difficult entry to the world.

My brilliant clinical psychologist asked me to write a very frank and honest memoir of my experience. He urged me to share my story because he had encountered hundreds of women who had similar stories but birth trauma is still a taboo.

January 20th 2004

I had really fat feet. I kept looking at them, they looked like Hobbit's feet and I couldn't stand on them for long. I was 10 days overdue and really tired. We had been up for two nights whilst I had been having Braxton Hicks contractions.

Nothing in my pelvis felt right, I had this clicky kind of pain which must have been the baby's head engaging. I was told the day before I was 4cm dilated everything was ready to go; I was just waiting for it to start.

The midwife unit called and as I stood up to get the phone my waters broke.

There was green stuff in my water so they told me to come straight in.

8.30pm:

My husband drove at a gazillion miles an hour to get me to the unit. I had booked a water birth with lovely music, drug free with no doctors around. As I was being bumped around on the motorway my contractions started.

The baby kept passing meconium so they told me I'd have to go to the local hospital.

The hospital put me in a private room with dimmed lights and we put some music on.

Norah Jones 'Come away with me' was playing. I leaned into my husband for a cuddle and we started dancing, slowly moving together. I started crying – fear, excitement, love, happiness, and I said to him with a smile, "We are going to have our baby today."

That is the last bit of joy I remember for a long, long time.

It turns out that the shock of everything going wrong stopped my contractions. They put me on a bed and strapped me to a heart monitor.

Eventually my contractions restarted and became more frequent but I was still only 4cm dilated.

They broke my backwaters and there was loads of meconium so they decided to speed up my contractions by giving me oxytocin. Once the drip was in my contractions started coming hard and fast. It was around midnight and I was in pain and really tired but again, I was *still* only 4cm dilated.

I start to realize my labour was spiraling out of control and I was scared.

They came to tell me I needed pethidine. I started to cry. I didn't want to have it, but the doctor insisted, so in it went. The next 3 or 4 hours were an unconscious blur as I tripped out on exhaustion, pain and pethidine. I remember sleeping and waking every 2-3 minutes to moan through a contraction and go back to sleep until the next one.

21st January 6.30am

I was woken up to be told that the baby's heart rate was dropping and so was mine. My body was giving up I was still only 4cm dilated and the baby was getting distressed.

Apparently instead of working with my body the baby had been kicking against the contractions and now my body was giving up. They needed to get it out or we would both die.

I don't remember being scared. I was too tired, nothing they said made sense because I was exhausted and drugged up and I just wanted this to stop so I agreed to the emergency caesarean and an epidural. I was so tired I couldn't see properly to sign the forms.

The epidural happened quickly and they prepped me for surgery. I was wheeled down to the operating room, there were loads of people waiting for me, I felt really embarrassed to be causing such a fuss.

They put me on the operating table and put the green screen up. My husband came in dressed in scrubs. He sat next to me and held my hand.

I kept trying to sleep, I couldn't keep my eyes open but the anesthetist said I had to stay awake. Apparently my heart rate was so slow, if I slept it could plummet.

I was aware of tugging and my body was being pulled all over the place. I kept thinking *I'm going to fall off the table*. Then they told me *she* was out and they were cutting the cord. She was 9lbs 2oz and swallowed a lot of meconium so they quickly took her away to clean her lungs out.

They took ages to stitch me up I kept phasing in and out of consciousness but my husband kept talking to me which I remember being really annoying because I just wanted to sleep.

I saw the nurses covered in blood, loads of it, which seemed weird and somehow registered as not right. Someone asked me if I wanted to breastfeed. I nodded yes.

I was wheeled out. Then nothing.

A nurse calling my name woke me up. I was sitting more upright now, in this quiet recovery room. The sun was streaming through the window but I was so tired I wanted to go back to sleep but the nurse kept talking to me and I wished she would stop.

I couldn't make my arms move, they were so heavy. They put her on me, skin to skin

I was scared she would fall and I couldn't stay awake so I asked them to take her. I found out later that my notes said, 'Mother broke contact.' I felt like a failure.

She didn't sleep that night. I was in so much pain I could barely lift her; I sort of dragged her from the cot and pulled her up by an arm and leg so I could feed her. We were not doing well. My colostrum wasn't keeping her full up and I was just so tired.

I had to shower and pull off my dressing. I couldn't stand up, my husband had to hold me up. It was horrendous. I cried as I pulled off the sticky plaster.

24th January

We were finally home. A midwife visited and told me I had a hemorrhage in surgery when they removed my placenta. I lost over a litre and a half of blood.

The next two weeks were a blur. I hated the crying, the feeding, the broken sleep. I was just exhausted and overwhelmed all the time.

After five weeks I decided I couldn't cope with being at home with her so I decided to go back to work

The next few months were awful. I was really stressed, I was trying to breastfeed, I was three stone overweight and exhausted. My body was a mess, the muscles in my belly were so stretched I still looked pregnant and the skin where they cut me hung down to my thighs.

I developed a massive kidney infection. I couldn't move and was given antibiotics. This was followed by a uterine infection and more antibiotics, colds, sciatica and bladder infections, until my doctor diagnosed me with post-natal depression and retrospective post-partum psychosis.

On New Year's Day I woke up hungover. I was lying in fetal position and crying. The mania was gone and the big black wave of depression had finally pinned me down.

The next three years became a daily battle to get out of bed and make it through the day. I was always exhausted.

I thought about killing myself a lot but I didn't have the energy to get up and do it. I was numb. I hated my life. I hated being a parent. I hated myself so much, I want it all to stop and go away and I just wanted to sleep. The tiredness never stopped.

I thought about leaving them both. They'd have been better off without me but I didn't know where to go.

June 2010

My daughter was a normal, happy, noisy six-year-old. We looked like such a happy family but I wasn't really her Mummy. I didn't do that stuff with her. I couldn't.

Truth is, I felt sick at the thought of doing things with her. I went through the motions, I played, I kissed her and cuddled her but something stopped me from loving her.

I felt I made a huge mistake and I was stuck with it. I didn't know how to love her. I felt like I didn't give birth, I felt she was taken out of me; I felt like such a fraud.

I sought out help from a clinical psychologist. He told me I did love her, the love was in my heart but there was just too much pain in the way for me to feel it, but that it was possible to come back from the darkness.

November 2016

I wasn't able to share my story for many years. It is only now that my daughter and I have created a beautiful relationship that I feel able to. The woman who went through this feels like a very different one to the woman I am now.

This is therefore dedicated to all the women and children who have experienced birth trauma, who feel isolated, lost, alone and worst of all, a failure.

If it helps even one woman realize there is hope and that there is no shame in what she has been through, it is worth it.

Chapter 32

Whatever it Takes

by Laura

At your darkest moments, you must find the light. I promise with all of my being, it is honestly there. Listen carefully to the quiet — not the loud roar of the voices in your head that tell you nothing but lies. Find the truth in the silence. You are necessary, you are loved, and yes, you are definitely worthy. Your strength will surprise you, your resilience will enable you and if you let it, your faith will carry and sustain you. Forever we are bonded the people who have fought off the insidious voices in our minds. The voices that tell us that we can make the pain go away; that we have a choice. There is only one choice that you can't make: giving up — because giving up is not an option. You will prevail, you will fight your way through this, and reaching for help is a great way to start. The voices are strong, but we are stronger. It just takes a bit of help. Help is sometimes necessary to find that strength. So reach out with all of your strength and courage with all that you've got; and whatever you do, don't let go.

I was born and raised approximately thirty-five minutes outside of Pittsburgh, Pennsylvania. I was raised loving God, loving people, loving laughter, and of course, loving the Pittsburgh

Steelers. I grew up with a brother six years older than me, and loving parents who were pretty much what you'd classify as the 'typical middle class family.' We had our fair share of pets, from turtles to hamsters, and of course, dogs. My love for animals only grew over the years, and it will always remain one of my passions for sure.

I was a very active child, who loved sports, was always outside, and was always on the go. So I carried my love of sports through the school years, as well as my passion for writing. As far back as I can remember, I was always writing.

In school, my teachers would say to me, "You are going to do something with this writing of yours someday." I never really took it seriously, but as I've aged, I have realized how therapeutic it has become for me.

My biggest passion, of course, is my family. I have been married to the same man for thirty-three years and we have raised two beautiful children together. My eldest has been married for ten years. She has no filter, but she is fun-loving and passionate about life. The best thing about her though, other than her love, is her two beautiful boys. They are the air in my lungs. My grandsons' laughter is what pushes the blood in my veins.

My son is twenty. He knows what he wants, and he goes after it. He has a sense of humor that is demented at times, but he is always hysterical, very intelligent, and extremely well-spoken. As far as my family, I am blessed. I've been blessed with beautiful family, friends, and even strangers that show kindness.

I tend to be attracted to real people, I don't go for the fakes; not to sound narcissistic in any way, I just don't have the time for fake people — they really can bring you down. I believe that a higher intervention places people in our lives at the right time and the right place. I smile to myself when I am reminded by that because he knows exactly what—or who—we need and when we need them. My smile and my laughter come through him along with all that there is, because he is my God, my father in Heaven, my savior. I have felt his presence too many times to question his truth, and I will forever honor and worship him, even though I know he has to have a sense of humor to love me.

As wonderful and breathtaking as life can be I have found depression is really what I consider 'the hard stuff.' Walking through depression is like walking through a huge vat of jello. You can't see, you can't smell, you can't function. I first felt the grips of depression when I started to notice a difference in my illness.

In late 2013, things were changing, and I was scared. Back in 2002, I was diagnosed with Lupus, an autoimmune disease that can attack your body at any place and any time. Essentially, Lupus cannot detect which cells in your body are good and which are not, so your body basically attacks itself all of the time. Luckily, there are new medications and research that are helping to find a cure, but unfortunately, that time hasn't come yet. Though, I am hopeful for that day.

Lupus can cause many debilitating symptoms, especially when it attacks major organs. Along with severe pain, crushing exhaustion, and flu-like symptoms several times a week, it has also gone into my central nervous system. Because of this, it has affected my ability to read and write, and I even have a hard time focusing during movies sometimes. This has had a major impact on my everyday life, including my ability to work. Lupus affects every single person differently. For some, it can have minor effects that make it possible to lead a pretty normal life. Others, unfortunately, are literally fighting for their lives. So briefly, one of my symptoms of Lupus that is linked to my central nervous system, is depression; and coping with that is like navigating the ocean without a compass. I also started having serious balance issues. I started grabbing onto desks, counters, anything. Then, one day, if I had not grabbed onto my marketing supervisor, I would have been on the floor. That's when I knew that I had a problem. Long story short, I was forced to give up my job. That's when things started to go downhill. I had lost track of almost everything in my life, including taking care of the house, my family, and myself.

The first time I thought about ending my life, I simply shook it off. It seemed like nothing until I was spending hours researching suicide. How to do it, how to not get caught, I had myself in training. *I was training to end my own life.* After all, I had the right to. My body had failed me and I was losing control of everything around me. I even started to get triggered with dark feelings by certain objects, places, or memories.

Everything around me became a weapon. It was horrifying. Hundreds of pills, serious injectable drugs, that didn't make me better, but I knew could take my life. Even cleaning products, knives, everything. Even our swimming pool was calling my name, begging me to come inside and have the cover suck me down. Before I knew what had hit me, I was watching myself give up, and it was sickening. I felt shame, anger, rage, fear...I truly felt like I hated myself.

Fortunately, I could not hold it in at my next doctor's appointment. I broke into tears. It ended up being a good thing though, because she was insistent that I needed help, and she was right. I didn't really want help from a therapist. I wanted to hate her. When I pulled up, there was one spot right in front of the building. It was a quick punch in the gut for me — it's what I like to refer to as a 'God wink.' It was meant to be. As soon as I talked to the therapist, I realized she was also a God wink. I was meant to meet her, and she was meant to help me.

Since that first visit, she has sat at the hospital with me, one time for eight hours almost. She has made me completely trust her, more importantly she has taught me to trust myself. She made me believe in reaching for hope. I don't hesitate too long anymore, and that's only thanks to her. You have to reach for help, it is the most courageous thing you can do for yourself. She has been completely real with me from the beginning, and I with her. I know in my heart, without crossing her path, I would not be here any longer.

I didn't realize that I had found myself in a place of complete despair, until the morning of my fifty-third birthday. It was the first time I knew that this was not just a floating thought. This feeling that was sucking the air from my lungs, literally crushing me from the inside out, broke me into something unrecognizable. I actually remember thinking that I would probably die right then and there because I was suffocating in the darkest sadness I had ever felt. Pain radiated through my entire body, and it felt like my head was going to explode. Yes, it was seriously true, I wanted to die. No more pain, no more losing control, no more emotional devastation to the people I loved. No more me.

I also recognize that watching or hearing someone go through those dark feelings is not an easy task. I only experienced it once; it was actually someone from our group. She posted on Facebook and even though I was in panic mode myself, I knew had to help her. Knowing that she was feeling that deep in despair made me sick to my stomach. No one should ever have to feel that way, especially alone. I think that the stigma that surrounds metal illness is very sad; people should not have to feel afraid to talk about it or seek help. I wish that people would take the time to consider that no one wakes up and thinks to themselves, *I want to wake up and feel suicidal today*, just as I'm sure that no one wishes for cancer or any other diseases. My heart aches for people that really duck away from this subject. Most likely, they do it out of fear, and truly they should feel fear. Depression, mental illness, or suicide can touch any of us, or worse, someone that we love, at any given moment. I get it, it's scary.

I am so grateful for my friends and all of my family. They are what gets me through the dark times. I used to think of missing out on the joy they would bring me, but in my newly found depression, I forgot about the joy I would bring them. So that's what I keep in my mind, *Do not take away their joy*. The joy that only I can give — because thankfully — there is only *one* of me. Now, I think about loss in not the terms of my losses, but the losses of the people I love the most. So now, for them, I fight, and I win.

Depression is wicked, it makes you want to run and hide. It turns you into someone who wears masks to the point where you don't even know yourself. You have to hold on to your loved ones and friends, and remember to turn to someone you trust, or someone that is professionally trained to help you when you need help. If you have a pet, hold on to them too. In my darkest moments, my dogs were my saving grace. They sensed my pain, I have no doubt about that. So hold them, their hearts are in the right place with you.

I hope there is something in my chapter that can help someone else. Remember to do the best you can, and you will stack up to God. Even if you slip, start climbing again; because the fight is *worth it*. So many times I have felt so completely alone during this struggle. People may not understand it, but I know in my heart,

God does. In fact, I would like to share one of my favorite bible verses.

She is clothed with strength and dignity, and she laughs without fear of the future.

- Proverbs 31:25

If I were sitting with someone who was suicidal right now, first, I would hug them, then I would tell them to avoid denial, it's the most dangerous thing you can do to yourself. Believe in yourself indefinitely, and *reach for help*. Trust in your faith, avoid being alone, be with someone you trust, and allow yourself to break. Broken things are easier to fix than you think, let the hurt out, and just one step of strength equals several in courage.

Thank you for the opportunity to share my story, may God's blessings be with you,

Laura.

Chapter 33

One Breath of Air

by Mia Zachary

"A tsunami is a series of [ocean] waves generated by sudden displacements [in the sea floor, landslides, or volcanic activity]. The tsunami wave may come gently or may increase to become a fast-moving wall of turbulen[ce]. Although a tsunami cannot be prevented, the impact can be mitigated through preparedness, warnings, and effective response.

– National Oceanic and Atmospheric Administration

If swept up by a tsunami, look for something to use as a raft.

- United States Geological Survey

My name is Mia Zachary. I am a mother, an award-winning novelist, a trademarked inventor, an entrepreneur, a teacher, and a spiritual healer. None of these accomplishments would have been possible had I not asked for help and accepted counseling. I recently celebrated my 50th birthday, something I never expected to live long enough to see. I am profoundly grateful that I have.

Everybody gets 'the blues.' That's a mild depressive state, a normal reaction to a loss, a natural response to grief. Depression with a capital D, however, is 'the blacks.' It's an overwhelming sense of despair and hopelessness that impacts or even impairs your ability to function. Because depression is what is known as an invisible illness, everyone's experience is unique to them and usually hard to detect. From the outside, it looks like 'moodiness,' 'quietness,' or being 'down in the dumps.' Inside, it manifests as persistent, overwhelming, smothering darkness.

You know that feeling when you're watching a scary movie or going through a haunted house? Or that feeling at the top of the roller coaster when you start to drop? Put those two feelings together and then imagine it doesn't stop. My own experience of depression, at best, was like the oppressive dread in the air when a thunderstorm is brewing. At the very worst, it felt like that tsunami... I might have had a bright smile pasted onto my face, but I wasn't waving "Hello"- I was trying to signal that I was drowning.

There is one thing above all else that I wish people who have never experienced depression would try to understand. Depression is not a sign of weakness. We're not stupid or lazy or unwilling to try. Because you can't see what's different about us, you can't know how hard we fight for our mental health every day. Anybody can give up- I almost did- it's the 'easier' thing to do. But getting out of bed every morning, holding back the desire to scream or cry, accepting the challenges of the day, and trying again... and again... and again?

That is not weakness.

Depression steals your energy; it robs you of motivation and holds you back; it keeps you small and insecure. Being raised by an abusive alcoholic father and a mother with a family history of depression had me believing that I was stupid and ugly, that I was never good enough at anything, and that I wasn't meant to be happy. Depression makes you want to hide, to avoid everybody, to retreat. For me, it was just easier to ignore the phone and say no to invitations and stop talking to people because I couldn't explain to them what I was going through.

Depression lies so often and so well that it finally becomes your personal truth. It's too much sadness for much too long. Depression feels like a massive weight on your shoulders, an incredible pressure on your chest. That weight gets heavier and heavier until it becomes pain. It leads to a slow death of the identity and, tragically, it can lead to a sudden death of the body.

Here's the thing, though: I never, ever, said I wanted to die; not even when I mixed oxycodone and metaxalone and set the world record for drinking an entire bottle of Chardonnay. All I wanted was to stop hurting. I wanted to stop feeling lonely and afraid, to stop feeling like a failure. I regret that someday my son will see this story and realize that, at one of the darkest times in my life, he wasn't enough to keep me around. Luckily, I will have to live with that and make the most of the time we could have lost.

Every one of us has a story and every one of our stories matters.

If you find yourself doubting that you can go on; think about how far you've come. Whenever you doubt you can face one more thing, remember what you've already survived. You are stronger than you know, braver that you think, and, yes, you can handle this emotional and mental challenge one more time.

Don't lose connection. Being alone inside of your own head is the worst place for you. Even if you don't ask for help directly, reach out to someone and just talk.

Don't lose time. Self-awareness is how you change your life, day by day, moment by moment. Allow yourself to feel whatever you're feeling- what we resist, persists.

Don't lose hope. H.O.P.E. stands for 'Hold on. Pain Ends.' Remind yourself of all that you have to feel grateful for. If that's too hard, be thankful for your next breath.

It's a Wonderful Life is a classic movie about a guy who is shown by his guardian angel what the lives of everyone in town would have been like without him. Who are your angels? Who will listen? Who can you count on? Who will hold your hand? Make a list to keep with you, a lifeline, if you will. I know, I truly know that it takes courage to ask for help. We worry about being judged or, worse, dismissed. Many of us hold on to our pain, afraid to reveal it. But people really do want to help; you just have to ask. There is power in courageous vulnerability.

Depression lies. But we're still here and we can rewrite our life story. Our stories matter. That's why, as hard as it has been to revisit, I had to share my story. I choose not to be ashamed of my past, to talk about it like any other 'dis-order' in the body. I believe that one message, or one story, or one hand reaching out, can save the life of one other person. The scars we try hardest to hide are the ones others need to see, so that they have permission to begin healing their own wounds.

The prefrontal cortex is the experience simulator. This is the area of the brain that, during your 'dark night of the soul,' projects your worst moments over and over again onto the screen of your mind. But I want you to understand that you *can* rewrite the story. This same area of the brain can help you imagine, and actually create, a life of sunlight and freedom and laughter and love. You have the power. You have always had the power, even though I know very well from experience it's hard to believe that.

If you've never seen *The Secret* DVD or read the book, the premise is that the law of attraction can be harnessed to change our lives. By thinking positively, we can attract health, money, happiness, or whatever we wish for by trusting in the universe- the author's neutral term for God. The power of positive thinking sounds like some hippy-dippy, airy-fairy nonsense, but there is scientific data to back up the metaphysical theorems.

Each morning, I make a decision about how I want my day to go. I count my blessings. I find things that make me feel good. I try to make someone smile. In other words, I've reprogrammed the chemistry in my brain to increase the levels of dopamine, oxytocin and serotonin- the 'love and happiness' neurotransmitters. Watching that DVD changed my thinking. Changing my thinking changed my life; saved it in fact.

As of this writing, I've had some bad days (usually whenever the sun isn't shining). That is just going to happen. I've had moments of anxiety or worry, felt the sadness of a loss, and wondered how the hell I was going to handle some issue that came up out of nowhere. That's just going to happen, too.

However, I am proud to say that it has been years since I've had a full-blown depressive episode.

Storms are always going to come through—predicted or unexpected— but I truly believe there will never again be a tsunami for me. By the grace of God, with the blessing of family, good friends and mentors, I've learned to walk between the rain.

Acknowledgment: not everyone comes out of the darkness alive. I want to thank each and every one of my co-authors for being strong enough to find a way through, and for being brave enough to bare a piece of their soul by contributing to this book project. I'm glad you're still here.

Chapter 34

Tears from Heaven

by Kristie Knights

I honestly do not know when it started, what could have been the trigger; but what I do know is that it lingers. It is a presence that swarms the depth of my mind more often than I care to share. I believe it always will. It is not so much the desire to die. Please do not get me wrong, there have been life experiences that spun me like a top; reeling, begging for mercy. But there hasn't been a time I looked to the heavens and truly wanted to die.

Death is peculiar.

It always has been for me. When I was a child, the first death I experienced was that of my grandmother. It was a tragic death. She was killed in a car accident by a driver that was intoxicated. I remember my mother receiving the call as if it was yesterday. The fear and panic enveloped the house.

I was the tender age of twelve. The details are colored in my mind for eternity. The next week was filled with pain, wailing, and sleepless nights. The day of the burial was etched in my mind. It was the final moment of the burial service that I cannot forget. As I stood at a distance from the coffin, I watched. The ability to release one's body is an act of both mind and body. Tears streamed down my face, nausea overcame me as I stared at my mother. Desperately, she clung to her mother's coffin. As she wept, calling out for her mother, loved one's gathered to stand vigil while she grieved. The tragic and sudden loss of my grandmother was more than she could withstand. My body ached, wrenched with despondency, I could barely stomach the agony and pain she surrendered to in that moment. The bellows of her pain were heart-wrenching.

My grandmother was killed at the age of 53. I could not tell you when the grieving dissipated. It plagued our home for many years to come. It was in those moments of dark sadness I wrestled with my own depression. My desire to escape the pain heightened after years of battling the demons in my mind.

As I have aged, the thoughts often echo in my mind…*What if*. It is the subtle suicidal ideation that can be haunting at times. When the nights are long and emotions raw, plans have been devised. *What if*… Do you know what I mean? What if I drove into the semi-truck on the highway? What if I jumped off the bridge? What if I killed myself? How would my family react? Would my friends be told? Would they care? How will my clients find out?

I have planned my funeral in my mind a thousand times over. I can hear the music playing, words unspoken, and devastation in the room. *What if*… There have been times in my life when the suicidal thoughts would intensify. Most often it was times I felt rejected, abandoned, or as if no one sees me. Perhaps you scoff, or are surprised by my story. Yes, I know. I am the eldest child. I am expected to be the strongest. I am a psychotherapist. I am expected to be the healthiest. Oh yes, I am a leader, I do not break. Screw you.

I was raised to be tenacious. I had no other choice but to be strong in my first marriage. In the darkest moments; I was angry, resentful, so tired of being strong. I couldn't bear to be strong another moment. I was expected to be strong, so strong for everyone. *What if…*

It was more than a year into the process of my divorce. I had vomited for days. In that moment I could not remember the last time I had mental clarity. Each day I fought to stay alive emotionally. I do not believe anyone truly knew the extent of the pain that engulfed me. I presented, well you know, strong. I was a force to be reckoned with. I was intentionally cold, a bitch. I feared nothing, with the exception of going back into the marriage.

This is not a story to destroy my ex or about the gritty details of a divorce. On this day, financial ruin was moments away. I could not breath again. The pain had become unbearable. I was strangled by his anger, and pursuit of revenge.

The day prior I had conceded to a large sum of money to secure the house in the divorce. It is my childrens' home. It is the home my father and I built together. Despite repeated recommendation to release the house, I refused. I could not. It represented so much more than just a house. It represented my strength, my fortress, my refuge; a safe-haven for the children and I. It is my dream home. There was no way in hell I was walking away from it, from my soul. The last two years building the home under the guise of a divorce proved to be empowering.

Regardless, I am detracting. My private practice was thriving, but I had nothing left to give clients emotionally. Each day I showed up, to be a warm body, but felt like a shell of a therapist. It seemed to go unnoticed by most, but my guilt and shame plagued me. On days I could not sustain, clients were cancelled. I would drive and drive for hours. Some days I would drive three hours one direction only to turn around and drive three hours back to my office. I told not a soul. Most often I drove to McConnell's Mills, a state park, and walked the trail. I spent hours sobbing, crying out to God in disbelief. I would beg for his mercy.

On this day I could not drive fast enough to relieve the pain. No matter the rate of speed, my head throbbed, my heart pounded, shame engulfed me. I smoked one cigarette after another. No, I was not a smoker. In fact, I am sure many who know me are quite surprised to read of such a behavior. I didn't care at the time. I searched for what would ease the pain, take the edge off.

Although I chose to leave my marriage, understand me, it was never what I had dreamt for my future, nor the future of my children. Every fiber of my being knew this was the best decision for myself, and my children. It didn't matter, the shame branded me daily. Day after day after day after day; *What if…*

Driving at speeds well over 110 mph I reached my destination. Often others would come to the park to hike or kayak. Sadly, accidental deaths had occurred at this location. *What if…*

 I sat in my car screaming. I do not know why really. At the time it was the rawest of emotions. I had failed. I failed my family, I failed my children. What was to remain in this life? Pain, hurt, angst. It wasn't worth it any more. I walked the trails in tears, in prayer. I wailed, much as my mother had; however, it was the calling of desperation to save my life, to save my mind.

I fell to my knees in the dirt. I could see my reflection in the water. I cried out, have mercy, have mercy; I cannot bear this pain any longer. I lay at the creeks edge, watching the water rush past me. The air was chilled despite the sun. I was alone. There was not a soul that I had seen. I could smell the dirt as I lay there. Who am

I? What have I done? What kind of person ends a marriage due to her own unhappiness? I began vomiting; shaking compulsively. I hated myself in that moment.

It was a dichotomy of emotions. I knew I had the strength; but knew I couldn't go on another moment enveloped in despair. I could no longer fight him, the system, my mind. I clutched the pills in my hand. My mind was flooded with images of my children. It was as if I was watching an old movie. I was terrified of myself. I was terrified of my thoughts. I was terrified of who I was in that moment. *What if…*

As I lay there in the mud, contemplating my own life, sickened by perceived selfishness; it began to rain. It was not forecasted. Pelted by tears from the sky, I felt at peace momentarily. All the world quieted. The chaos in my mind ceased. As I rolled over to look at the sky a dove flew overhead. Without intention, I released the pills into the water. Inhale life, exhale death.

Driving was lack luster; perhaps numbing. My thoughts raced in confusion, bathed in clarity. I do not remember a conscious decision to go to a church. It wasn't until I entered the church I realized where I had been led. It wasn't even my church. It was an open church.

I recall sitting in the last pew, dripping, face stained of mud, and chilled. As I prayed, I wept. But you see, they were tears of joy. They were tears of redemption, grace, and love. That day the rain washed over me, made me anew. The transgressions I saddled to my back were absolved. As the dove flew over me, it was a very intentional sign of God's love for me. A dove is often portrayed as a sign of peace and love. A dove is a messenger. It delivers a message and returns home. Since that day, a dove has come into my space multiple times. Often it has appeared on some of my most difficult days. It is a reminder that I am unconditionally loved, and never alone.

As time passed, the divorce was finalized. Healing has been a journey back to myself. Just as the dove, no matter the message, it returns home. I have returned to my soul. It is a place of service to others. It is a place of purpose. Live a life of purpose, of service. Within that space you will discover healing and freedom.

UnSung Heroes

I want to say a prayer for the people I know,

my family & friends, even those on TV shows

For people in far-away lands I'll never see,

& the neighbors I don't know who live right near me

For those who are injured, alone, or ill,

those who have given up & lost their will

For those who right now are suffering & struggling,

trying to keep their heads above water with all they are juggling

For those in dark places who have lost their way,

or those with no voice who feel they have no say

If I could give everyone love, joy, & peace I'd do it in a heartbeat,

I'd clothe the cold, get the homeless off the streets

I'd stop every violent person before they hurt a child,

I'd help endangered animals remain free & wild

I'd listen to everyone's stories because they're simply amazing,

I'd spend an entire day watching the beauty of animals grazing

I'd thank every veteran & their families for my freedom,

I'd try to inspire our youth & help to lead them

I'd cheer on all the underdogs with my big, loud voice,

I'd try & help those who feel they have no choice

I'd cure all the disease or at least try to ease pain,

I'd help everyone with their financial strain

I'd lend my hand, my shoulder, or my ear,

I'd try to help anyone if I were near

But I'm only one person, no different from you,

So I put my faith in God's hands because He knows what to do

I say these things to him almost every day,

When I thank him for my blessings & he listens while I pray

If you haven't talked to him for a while, I can tell you this,

I've been praying for you & your family too because you're all on my list.

Amen.

-Jessica D. Comer

Conclusion

We often spend our time engulfed in the lives of others; whether it is through social media, or the community gossip center. We watch from a distance; just a glimpse is all a person needs.

Between the pages of *UnSung Heroes: Deconstructing Suicide through Stories of Triumph* the contributing authors shared their darkest moments when life didn't seem worth living to them. As the stories unfolded, it became clear they are truly heroes! They surmounted all tragic life experiences, stressors, and mental illness; such as depression and anxiety. It was and most cases still is an internal battle defeat daily. This is often the case with most people who live with a mental illness.

See, life is worth living. Most think that thought should be second nature. But what you see is just the opposite. Many struggle with the darkest of thoughts. The shame associated with the thoughts is overwhelming due to the lack of awareness of not only mental illness, but suicide. It just isn't talked about. Instead, the stigma and shame breeds sadness, depression, lies, and loneliness. The stigma must be destroyed so those who struggle may feel safe to share. Through sharing is healing. Through healing we will see a direct correlation of a decrease in the number of people who die by suicide.

Suicide is preventable. The primary purpose of this book was to provide a platform for those who have struggled with mental illness to shine. My intention with this book is to shine a spotlight on those who have survived the darkest hours of their lives. Each person has value. Often the value is desecrated through others, and life experiences. When this occurs; it is a life left fighting a battle alone.

Mental illness and suicide is a taboo subject in our culture. This has led to increased shame and hiding of the battle within for so many. The opportunity to share their story provides a voice for the pain. It validates that what they experienced was very raw and real. It gives them the place to embrace who they are and the inspiration they bring to their world. It gives them the chance to find purpose in their pain. Each story will save lives. I have no doubt at all.

In fact, as the authors were writing their stories, there were often remarks of "Thank you, I have never told my story before." Or, "I pray my story and all of this pain saves a life; just one life and it is worth it." The level of courage and vulnerability required to publish a person's darkest hour is humbling, don't you think?

The art of telling your story, a life experience or struggle, is cathartic in nature. There is an intense healing property in giving words to the pain. In addition, continued empowerment occurs when the story is shared publically. UnSung Hero Publishing will continue to create a platform for those who struggle with a mental illness, or experienced a traumatic life event. It will give space for the pain, validate the journey, and give rise to the healing. A true hero experiences battle. Each author has battled and won over the skeletons within.

The second purpose of this book is to destroy the stigma around mental illness and suicide. It is a call to action for suicide awareness and prevention. This is a unique method to deliver the education and awareness to eradicate suicide. A portion of this book, and all books published by UnSung Heroes will be donated to the awareness and prevention of suicide.

It is very powerful for those who battle with mental illness and suicidal thoughts to have a platform to inspire others to live, and to give the hope of leading a life of purpose and joy as they are!

There is no greater gift you can give another than showing value to another human being. The greatest way to show value is to accept who they are, warts and all. There is not space for judgement or condemnation. But instead, of love and acceptance, despite their struggles.

Thank you for supporting those you love in your life that may struggle with mental illness or suicidal thoughts. Through your presence in their life, and the purchase of this book; you are saving lives!

If you, or someone you know has been affected by mental illness and suicide and would like to be featured by sharing story in the next upcoming book in the UnSung Heroes series please visit www.iriseleadership.com for more information.

'In the darkest hour, you are not alone. Just reach for me and I will be there. You are an unsung hero in disguise, waiting for light to shine. Regardless of your path, you are worthy of love divine.'

- KK

iR;se

UNSUNG HEROES

Life is the greatest story to be told. As each author unearthed their soul, it is with great purpose. The rate of suicide is the highest it has been in 30 years. Suicide is the number one cause of death for children aged 10-21. This is not a mystery. It is preventable. The key to successful eradication of suicide is through the destruction of the stigma of mental illness.

With courage, vulnerability, and candid truth by unsung heroes; pain was given a voice. It is through the validation of the pain, permitting the sharing of thoughts despite the pain, that will alleviate the shame. Shame and judgement deter honesty and healing. Do your part to save a life.

Have you been affected by suicide? Do you struggle with thoughts and shame? Have you lost a loved one to suicide? You are not alone. Do not fear telling your story. Do not fear reaching out for help and support.

Just the loving acceptance of another will save a life. Just a word or act of kindness can save a life. Do not wait until it is too late. You can save a life.

If you or a loved one has been affected by suicide and would like to be featured in the next UnSung Heroes book, please send an email to kristie@kristieknights.com. In the subject line please type: Book Project.

Should you desire to discover how you can donate or be a part of the iRise community, please go to www.iriseleadership.com.

If you are in need of a professional speaker in the area of suicide prevention and awareness, please contact the iRise Leadership Institute.

The End